At the gates of the soul – dew drops on the skin

Sirpa Pursiainen
2016

© Sirpa Pursiainen
Translation and editing: Christine Puza & Sirpa Pursiainen
Cover and paintings: Sirpa Pursiainen
FACE training center
deepway.fi

At the gates of the soul – dew drops on the skin

Sirpa Pursiainen
2016

Foreword

I met Sirpa in London in the fall of 2001, when it seemed that half of the European Continent and United States were converging on the city for the wedding of a mutual friend. We were thrown together quite by accident, but quickly became fast friends as we explored the city together. As I got to know her, both then, and throughout our correspondence and visits over the years that followed, I discovered in her a woman of great depth and insight. Her gifts are spiritual yet practical. She is a person deeply invested in the betterment of the world, with a carefully attuned understanding of the beauty and complexity of its many relationships.

Storytelling is an important therapeutic technique, with benefits well established in the psychological literature. We are healed through words, as we tell our own stories, or listen to those told to us. A well told story can produce insight, correct a cognitive distortion by seeing a situation in a new way, or providing context for an unusual feeling or happening. Stories use metaphor and imagery to change the way we see our lives and the world, offering healing and growth to everyone - teller and listener alike. They connect us to each other and help us find meaning and hope. Therapeutic storytelling can change the way we see our lives and the world. Using personal symbols and allegory, stories offer healing to everyone.

Across all cultures, from the petroglyph to the e-mail era, stories have been told to communicate knowledge and wisdom. Over and over again I have seen others find deeper meaning and purpose as they examine their own personal history though the lens of creative storytelling. By replacing unhealthy narratives with new ones through the reframing of their experience, destructive patterns of relating and being can be released, paving the way for growth and new levels of understanding.

Here Sirpa has woven a richly imaginative and symbolic tale that illustrates the healing process on a deeply personal level. Each member of the family portrayed examines their own wounds of the past and comes to understand the impact of their familial legacy and how it affects their ability to relate to themselves and each other.

As I worked with her over the past year to perfect the manuscript and refine the finer points of the translation, we made every effort to balance the necessary flow of the narrative with an openness that would appeal to many different meanings. It was important for us to allow many ways to infer the symbology of the text and leave it open for a truly personal experience.

After many months of steady work, Sirpa Pursiainens' insightful foray into therapeutic storytelling has grown into this inspiring book. I am confident that her wisdom, imagination and generosity will help to kindle the healing process within you. It is our sincere hope that by following these characters as they grow and change along the many travails of their path, that their story will bring you solace and a new understanding of yourself, your life, and others.

Christine Puza, Editor/Translator

Contents

Introduction 8

TOGETHER ALONE 11
Trilogy 12
Pike-perch of the warm waters 14
Magpie at the cats' bowl 17
Travesty 18

THE WAY OF MAN 21
Chase of the nightmares 22
Cuttlefish 23
Insurmountable mountains 25
Socrates decorating swords evoke 26
Lost 29
Yearning 32
Singing horses 34
The garden of One-eyed 36
Birds and the fishes 38
Swirls in my own ocean 39
Hamleti´s treasures 41
Equivalence of time and occasions 44
Grandpas' field 45
    The mill 45
    Bad weather 46
    Grandpa at the gates 46
    Grandpas' Iron Youth 47
    Grandpa´s death 51
Child in me 53
    The Ruined fence and the falling star 53
    Fishes underneath 57
    Dragonfly 59
The son 62
    Water will bear 62
    A Funny Dream about the Royal Family 64
At the gate 66
    A man of his time in space 68

WOMANS' GETAWAY 71
Blood runs in a goblet 72
Discovering the scene of legitimate murder 73
Pain 75
Behind the bars 76
The forest 77
Wise men of the time 79
The ways of the fire 81
A cooling air 82
The heritage 84
    Father *84*
Waterlily 86
Wolves 87
Farewell 88
    Goodbye *88*
    Funeral *89*
    So long! *90*
Lapland 92
    Pakasaivo *92*
    Preacher *94*
    He creates everything to be new *95*
    Under the snow *96*
At the fountain 98
    Water over the path *98*
    Water of the fountain *99*
    In the meddle of the dark *101*

AT THE BRIDGE 104
The carrier of fire 105
Eyelids 106
Internal resonance 107
Arched bridge 108
Under the skin 109
Becoming united forest 110
Afterword 112

Introduction

When the minds' arcs
are running out as tears
at the gates of the soul,
angels are waiting.
With open arms they welcome
the seekers of motherland
who are lost in the forest with tick tack bells
where stones has turned out to metal
and unnaturals has forgotten to be the treasures of travellers.

Water rises up from the flow
to praise the heavens,
to admire the clouds
who reach to offer food for the hungry
from the banquet table of the air flow,
with new containers.

No one wants to be away
from that moment.
No one who has dared to swallow the silver
of the mirrors reflection.
or who has drunk their own outlines from the water level.
To be as who you are
is the strongest evidence of being human.

That is when the identity of all the wounds are revealed
and all the odysseys will get their names
at the chain of the memories.
Every meaningful meeting and abandonment
will rest in peace within the furrows of the hands.

That is time when hair
can flutter in the air
and it will bring dew drops for the skin.
Is it only this life
between birth and death?
Or did there appear a living plant after all?

Yes,
the wind brought a seed for the cold water.
Dew gave a birth for it
and the heat fostered it for ownership.
To be in everyone´s lips, as in meeting.
To be a guide for travellers of midnight.

To encourage those who are hiding in darkness,
the composer for those who have forgotten
the songs of their names.

This entire is one of the victories of brightness
at the celebration of the starry sky and solar system.

TOGETHER ALONE

Trilogy

"How long have you been looking through that gap in the blinds?"
- "I don´t know. Most of my life."

"I'll put the tea on, you can get the rest of your thoughts."
- "I should get my thoughts for somewhere else? That´s what I've done all my life, this is much more important."

 "Watching children play, huh? Who would want to spend their time like that?"
- "If only I still had that, who I was. I would be again who I really am. But so much has been lost along the way."

I walked silently into the dining room. I paused for a moment in front of the hall mirror. I did not want to say anything more. Tea water would boil in time. In it´s own time. I sat down to wait.

Tea water vibrated and sang like thousands of moons and stars in the sky. The entire universe folded in on itself, an infinite circle, and he imagined the edges for it. Like it certainly had edges. Even if a person could not comprehend it, could not find them or had not seen the limits. But it had to have edges, unless that was the great himself. Or is potential limited at all for the great himself? Would he be able to create another unlimited and infinitely and still control it? Would it be like the moon, whose roots can dance and sing in the sea and in the air at the same time? He closed his eyes. Then you could see the sound what the ear will not dare to hear when spoken.

Our son had grown. We ourselves were mostly the same as we had been before. However, we had begun to turn away from each other. We lived together but alone, and had started to build our own worlds. Our eyes glanced only as far as ourselves, and our own desires, so that in the end we saw nothing. We had, however, our son, a so very innocent child. He had the courage to ask again and again, wanting to know more about the world around him. However, all of us were still one of the same; we needed to know that we are loved from time to time. We told our boy that he was loved, but because of the selfishness and indifference we did not say it to each other. Mornings blessed the nights, the nights blessed the days and none of us were paying attention to the respective moment.

Pike-perch of the warm waters

"Father, why did you go fishing at night, while I was sleeping? What fish did you catch?" My son rubbed his eyes and I could not tell whether he was tired or tearful. He was clearly annoyed that I did not give him permission to stay up so that he could have been able to come fishing with me. But the truth of the matter was that he would not have had the strength to stay awake.

"I was fishing pike-perches. Pike-perch feed on the surface of the water in bay coves on warm summer nights. Spinning of the lure must be timed with the line on the reel so that the fish will strike on the bait. Bait depends of the colour of the water. For our fuzzy lake I selected the bright bait. Pike-perch is like a chasing a wolf; it is bad to attack it directly, but you can drive their prey from behind for a long time.

Pike-perch doesn't fight at all, and that´s the reason why some people are surprised that there really is a fish on the line. Fishing pike-perches is exciting because catching it is more challenging than with many other fishes. "

My son listened intently to my story, but I knew that he was curious and had many more questions.
"Why do pike perch comes to the surface of the lake to eat only during the warm summer nights?" he asked.
I had to answer that I do not exactly know. I added, however: "Perhaps it is a self-indulgent mild fish. As the water gets colder it will swim to a warmer ground water. "
I knew that he would have more questions and I answered with impatience, even before I heard the questions. "Pike-perch looks similar to a long perch. The name of the species, *Lucioperca,* means actually the pike-perch.

There used to be a lot of pike-perches in Finland's inland waters in the early part of the 19th century. It has been less common for a long time as the waters have become more acidic as a result of forest drainage. That´s why pike-perches has been stocked in inland waters." But before I got chance to explain what stocking fish in lakes entails, my son had already asked for it.

"The fish are helped to reproduce and grow and then fishes are put into the lakes to help increase their numbers. Since then, pike-perch are expanding their territory and live in large schools. In Finland, one fish has been known to live for 28 years, but who's to say how old the rest of them have gotten! "

My son was clearly not interested in my story any more. He began to make movements of a fin with his hands. I still kept talking. I told him:
"I'm going to sell the fish I caught, as the pike-perch is valuable, so I will get a good price. I will buy a new lure with that money, because sometime soon there will be a magical night when the pike-perches will rise back to the water surface as a great collective. The whole surface of the lake will buzzing with fish. I will take some of them for us. But it's not known yet when this night will happen."

Now my son imagined he was a giant pike-perch and he ran back and forth with arms outstretched, pretending to swim. I mused, deep in thought. I thought about pike-perches and their adaptability to live in brackish water. I also thought about how the male fish will dig a spawning pit at an astounding 3 meters' depth and how strongly it defends the development of its young. Maybe my son´s play was a similar pit for him, built for safety.

The brutally honest thoughts, which I had had at the lake returned. I was tired of having to present the appearance of a happy father to my son. Sure, I felt immense happiness in his company, like all fathers likely experience. However, I notice my grip on my optimism slowly slid down into discouragement. My marriage was no longer the same. I sensed something else, too.

My wife was often on long business trips away and she always seemed to be increasingly more in distance. First I tried to explain the situation away with her work-related stress but the atmosphere became more tensed, even through the holiday season. I admitted to myself that I no longer knew her. I focused on myself and I started to compete in the amount of work in relation to the amount of work of my wife. I experienced a great deal of pride in my manhood that I was able to bear greater responsibility financially. However, the gorge between us only deepened.

What happens
as your hands are falling down.
You look at the reflection from the others' face
and you do not recognize it to be yours any more.

What happens
as the time makes the wall too high to get over.
The past will grab on to someones hand
and will carry it all, passing you from the distance.

What happens,
when the wind cannot sing its' song no more.
When the sight of it has gone too quiet
and it can no longer carry the words.

What would happen
if your eyelids would rest for a while?
To have the ego in selfhood
to be at home in human Being.

Let them walk through the frested years,
if that is their will.
Let them be blinded by the marsh tea,
if that´s where they walk.

What does it have to do with you, after all;
Only a few reflections on the grooves of your skin.

Magpie at the cats' bowl

Cat wanted out again for the night, and patted a mark on the Venetian blind with its paw. I let it out and I took out its' water and the food bowl. Cat ate for a few moments, then ran away to explore the environment. It was natural for a cat to save a bit of food for itself until it will get hungry. In fact, I went to bed. In the morning, the cat would run back inside, as it always has.

The night arrived. Cat hid itself in the bushes on the slope, and slept there between times. Magpie arrived at the cats' bowl. First Magpie gently grabbed the food in its beak, but it became more and more bold. Cat woke up and sneaked into the edge of a bush, and saw how food container food decreased. Cat did not dare to come out of the scene to get rid of the magpie. It just followed nearby, how his food was vanishing.

A second magpie arrived on the scene and their laughter steadily increased. Now they were fighting with each other for the cat food. The noise became so loud that it woke up a sleeping human being.

So I did wake up and, opened the door. Magpies flew away and the cat walked over to look at its empty food bowls, tail between its legs. "Yes, it would be far better to offer its dinner inside", I noted, for the cat.

Travesty

Could it all have been able to prevent? I do not know. I guess there where causes and faults with both of us; however the fact was that her acts went that far. This was all grotesque, so absurdly grotesque. Had the few beautiful words gotten her to feel and to act differently? I guess a beautiful woman knows she is beautiful, isn´t that needless to say? I guess the contract to be together means more than words of love? Am I even the father of our son?

The letters silently emptied themselves of their words. I opened my mouth, and I heard no voice with my ears. Lost a faith in miracles. Phone dropped from my hand, I did not get the assistance requested. I felt to the ground wondering what happened to me.

Lost a faith in miracles. I consoled familiar people through the glass wall. I cried my weeping inside. The consolation I got was that I knew something pure and real had been there before. Lost a faith in miracles.

Noise and silence was playing in the ears. Blood was moving, but something interfered with my thinking. I felt as if I were being pushed out of my body. I looked at myself from the outside. I do not know how long it took. I saw myself lying in the ground, without being able to help myself. Some part of me, however, was with hilarious mind, that part of me did not hurt at all. Until the pain came over my head, feeling came back into my body. I just thought I had lost my faith in miracles. I made it alive! Sometimes *no* does mean a later date, *maybe* might mean in a different way. Then I saw without hearing, now I can hear without seeing. I would no longer be a husband.

When I managed finally to get on my knees, anger filled the whole of my being, and I gave it to include:

> What are the words at skin of travesty,
> what are the trembling reaching
> of the roots of the wood.

What are the dunghills under the stars
and what is this whisper of death;
the word of selfishness.

That´s where the boats are falling apart
as the capacity of water-bearing deceive.
Above with arrogant pillars
which are protecting their own grounds.

That´s where the lies wraps around
capacity of sight of the eyelids.
That´s where the human mind
tunes its sparks.

Water runs still under the desert,
with poisoned snakes as crowns.
Power of oneself over his shoulders,
conjures own truth up into the sky

Why cannot you hear in silence
what humanity whispers with the wind?
Are you not able to look up the sky without sound
to see arc of the sky on the top of your head?

But there are only few who have the courage.

That is the will of the mind
who makes the lights and the shadows
for the view.

The word so vile,
lance of the heart.
Outfits of the gorge,
the enemy of its own.

With the other weather
and on the other sea,
word so light as feather,
tingling and unmistakable.

But there are two foxes at the nest,
begging to travel with,
to travel on their paths
to wallow at their gardens!

THE WAY OF MAN

Chase of the nightmares

The nightmares did not have time to reach me, because I held them firmly in my gaze with my eyes fully open. After the divorce, I was focused on my work. In the evening, the pressure upon me made me sweat, but still, my eyes were frozen.

Tomorrow at work I'll have to solve this problem ... today I tried this solution, it is solved in this section. Logically, alternatively, tomorrow I could try to continue the mix of A + B. Perhaps, however, AB would be a better.... No, because it can also affect the partition J. I turned over onto my ribs and pulled the blanket tighter around me.

I have to get some sleep. I wonder how much time has already gone by. How many hours could I get, if I fell asleep now? Not enough. I will never get enough sleep. I cannot sleep. No, I have to get some sleep. Well, maybe I could use my time more usefully... Could it be A + B + D? We tried that as a solution once. I wonder what was name of the system. Oh, I do not remember anything! Again, the entire night passes while I continually monitor my thoughts. *Where could I find the name of the system? Should I get up to look for it? No, now I have to sleep. I'll check in the morning. Well, what time is it now? When will I have to wake up?*

Finally, my eyelids dropped and I was asleep with this mantra. At least until a few hours later when I wake suddenly, thinking: *what is the name of the system*? I get up to read; a book about dreams, anything that could release me from this hell. For me, those are outreached dreams, because I've wallpapered my eyelids with an endless nightmarish treadmill of questions. I run towards sleep night after night, continually creating new labels for that internal wallpaper.

Cuttlefish

I had labored on the stone streets for so long that I had changed into a Cuttlefish. I could easily transform within the situations of the present and play any new role well. I found that I changed my color easily after listening to anothers' story for a while. I gave up being who I am. I thought I was an individual but in reality I was just like any other Cuttlefish with a ring-shaped large brain, possessed of only 30 per cent of its nervous system. The largest part of the nervous system prepared to respond to attacks and disguise.

Rush requirements of the others were as turbid as the muddy ocean floor. I had lost the ability to distinguish sea horses from the corals. But the nails of my tongue were able to catch up with the boasters, if necessary. My three hearts made it possible for me to live my three lives at the same time and still separately. The past, the future, and this moment. I distinguished pain and pleasure far apart - so I learned to act.

But I didn´t realize by that time that my blue blood was running through them all. I did not yet understand that the excreting of the ink, the works of my stomach, also runs through my brain.

However, as I got older I began to see more clearly the vibrations of the blood and water on the stone streets. I saw my own face as in secret and by stealth. I knew that after I reveal myself, it would be easier for others to identify me. It was time to be honest with myself.

So tired I am,
can you see it?
Traveled too much in place.

This thoughts are
just spinning now.
I do not get a grip to grasp.

Listen to me,
be nearby.
Require, do nothing, I ask.

My mind whispers:
All strength is leaving me.
My walk is futile.
Words will remain in my throat.

Tears are
disappearing now.
Anxiety clearing the space.

A never-ending,
Man, so tired.
Questions wondering.

Non-continuing,
grief over beyond
Do not know, who am I?

My mind whispers:
All strength is leaving me.
My walk is futile.
Words will remain in my throat.

My mind whispers:
All strength is leaving me.
My walk is futile.
Words will remain in my throat.

I no longer wanted to be a three hearted chameleon. I wanted to drink a glass of wine in peace. I wanted to breathe a sigh of encrypted prayers. I wanted the water to know me.

Insurmountable mountains

Insurmountable mountains loom before me. Simply the height and width of something like that is viscerally massive. Down in the valley it was sweltering hot. When you were out there you would constantly long to cool yourself in the small river in the valleys' floor. High above, in turn, it was cold, snowy and breathing was difficult due to lack of oxygen.

I writhed in my thoughts and my blood was pumping adrenaline through my entire being. I felt my heart throbbing rapidly inspite of the hot air. I just had to keep walking towards it.

I knew that after I had climbed up those peaks and landed there again, I would enter into the secret garden where my soul would be dancing free. I should set aside the time to prepare, to pack my backpack with all the madness, all the fear, all the time gone by, and all the future. I would need every bit of these on this path of humanity to find the Gate of Souls.

I knew I would be asked to dismantle my backpack once I was there, to get my change to look over the Fountainhead. The Fountainhead would not just reflect back, but also absorbs all that is unnecessary. It will strip and expose myself to myself, to see, who I was when I was born. That's why this trip is worthwhile.

Yes, it is worthwhile, even though there are surely men and women who have traveled here as well. They have traveled their own paths with prejudice, and without, to make unknown paths into words and sentences. But I decided to take responsibility for my own trip. Others will be the interpreter of their own. But the road before you, once known, might feel strange and unfamiliar.

Socrates decorating swords evoke

Travel seemed impossible. Each descent followed by ascent. My backpack was heavy. I walked forward without paying attention to where my feet would lead. The mountains seemed too far away to pursue. I was not paying attention to how I felt the steps, even though I watched the trailing surface of the street with some thought, so that I would not stumble. I arrived to the suburbs. Some alcoholic was resting on the pavement next to a building. I glanced at him carelessly. But then it happened, something that had not happened in months. This object, which was lying on the ground, spoke to me.
"Who are you? What are you doing here? "

"I am no one," I replied, "I do not do anything here. I am as long as I am. I'm sorry. "I thought I would get to continue my meaningless journey, but I was wrong.

The alcoholic spoke again:
"I am lost here. My journey was long and time and events too incomprehensible. I am Socrates. Do not think that I will let you go very easily. Can it be a coincidence that you are the first "no one" I've met in the current prevailing time? The coins of your mind seem to be running low! I think I am happier than you to be here. Are you a servant without the tasks of the servant?"

My mind stopped spinning around my own self and the misery of my life. Socrates did not allow it. After all, Socrates could not actually be in front of me, could he?

When I did not answer, Socrates continued.
"What do you people appreciate at this time? When you reap the harvest? Where are the gates of the way where you may meet each other? "

Now, my eyes were opened, I was open for discussion.

"We do have a lot of gates, but far less of meetings," I said. "People just go through the gates, here and there. Faceless machinery collects the harvest and metal and electricity makes the food out of it. Man only monitors and controls the events. But what do we value? What we have been told to: money, power and glory."

Socrates looked at me pityingly. "Harvesting is one of the most celebrated events of year´s cycle. How do you replace the joy of the harvest? Are all of you the kings and lords? How a servant and a slave receive its meaning, since there remains for him envy and disappointment in that setting? Yes, you seem to be just the servant, supplied free of duties. You have forgotten the importance of the gates. What on earth has happened? What wars you have had against humanity and divinity?"

Socrates' words were like swords; they raised me up out of months of the apathy I had been caught in. I realized that I had given up without noticing it and I had forgotten how to reason within myself. My own answers were only resonances led by leading questions. I replied to Socrates, why the coins of my mind seemed to be running low:
"I have been in the wars between people recently. Or actually I did not participate in the wars, others were, those who conquered. But, overall, I lost and therefore I remained alone. My wife went with other man and took our son with her. Now, there is nothing left that moves in me anymore. Nothing."

Socrates
"And what happens, does this not seem to feel real to you any longer?"

I replied: "Well, the steps of my feet are certainly irrelevant, meaningless. But how do I find the gates you mentioned? "

He said:
"That's what did not happen,
might not happen now.
What you dream about,
may take the form of the new.
What you fear,
must accompany you until you tame the fear.
You can redirect the steps,
- Even within each moment of today. "

I wandered through the harvest feast as I started again to walk. I was reminded of the words of my grandmother: "Whatsoever a man sow, that shall he also reap." I had sowed my mind with dejection and hopelessness. On the other hand while the priest had preached: "You shall cut it, that what someone else has sown."

Had I given a place for fruit to grow on the ground of my soul? Perhaps I had, but only for rotten grapes. I had given the words of discipline to grow, words which had created my fear. I had tried to cover the field of the fear, protect it from frost and all this had created prospects and apathy. After these weeds it was clear that even without words that kind of exclusion to your own life was too easy to play. I was the boy who had survived, but with stony bread in the pockets.

Bitterness had celebrated at party of destruction. To die for itself had been a pale and wavering contour beneath the surface of the water, until I ceased to be present. Escape from itself was not to be as whole as the small piece of time in my corner, clenched tight in my hands like blood dripping off. I had been the savior of myself for judging others, and judging myself to misery. Without a name it is easier to justify cruelty of indifference. But the many remaining questions still plagued me. Could I someday still rejoice at the harvest time? What battles I had gone against humanity and divinity?

My cup was overflowing with bitterness, as I pitied myself and warmed my hands in the ashes of yesterday. The paintings of my soul were covered in dust and darkness. Could I dare to take the liberty to see again? Could I see better if I could only paint a new scene? But what if I cannot? On the other hand, child can do it too.

Could I still own the kingdom of heaven? Could I still become a child who will ask, who is looking to learn, who rejoices, who dares to rely on the other as fears? Could I become a child who calls for a trust, who loves, who laughs, who cries?

I had been indeed a servant without duties to do. I wanted to change my lord. I knew I wanted to find more and more a man inside me, created by God. I have to find the gates, Socrates mentioned. Somehow.

Lost

But hope seemed to shrivel behind the shadows, the will turned down certainly as the sunsets. I was lost. I had already given up hope, because I did not know exactly what I was looking for. All the mountains were lost. Was the goal even important?

Mist floated above the swamp and I sensed the moisture of it. Tears streamed down my cheeks and rinsed the furrows and the years on my hands, which had stuck on to me. The swamp under me somehow allowed me to walk on it. This place was like the moments of the years I had lost. They had been so full of prosperous moss, so soft, so well accompanying me. Finally I sat down on the moss and I sighed deeply. In that moment I saw my home built in front of my eyes, a vision. I sighed with relief: finally I could rest!

The breath of the death greeted through the door´s keyhole as I stepped on the stairs. My home was empty. There were skeletons in front of the dining room table. They had had a feast going on. Grape clusters cried out for mercy and salvation at the fingers of one of them. Another skeleton´s long hair reached, all the way to the floor. Third one poured wine. Wine drops, frozen with the air, cried for the mercy of death. In the bedroom were more skeletons, who held onto the blankets as the pictures and moments of dream were singing the song of sorrow, begging for mercy. One of the skeletons in the living room had kept its other eye and followed closely the situation without being able to say anything.

I noticed that on living room sofa one of the skeletons still had one eye. It followed the situation closely, watching.

Still, this was my home. I would show the one-eyed how I would free the food out of skeletons control, how I would call the wine back to the glass and then on the palm of my hand. I would show the one-eyed how the lamentation of my dreams would sing on my cheeks. I would win my home back to myself and I would ask the one-eyed to handle my wooded garden. It would take care of the memory of buried skeletons.

As I had emptied my apartment of the skeletons I sat down in front of the window. A little fairy flew on my forefinger. The fairy began to tell me a story, one about a boy who got lost in the woods.

"The boy had gone out to the forest. He had seen so many interesting stone boulders and great climbing trees that he eventually became lost. Eventually, it got dark and the boy sat down on a stone. Then he heard singing and laughter and he had seen as the small campfire made a bit of light from a great distance. He was able to see it all as he was quiet, and no longer tried to look the same way back. The boy walked toward the fire and saw animals of the forest around a campfire.

There they were chatting, squirrels and foxes, hedgehogs and eagles, bears and waxwings. They winced for the moment as they saw the boy. But after they realized that boy was just a young boy and small in size, they greeted him kindly. The boy told them that he was lost and needed a place to stay. Animals of the forest promised to help him to build a tree house.

They built together the shelter for of the boy. The boy had always dreamed of that kind of shelter but he had never built one. Animals of the forest helped him to get the shelter to be strong enough. Tired boy climbed up into his tent, accompanied by a small squirrel.

Before going to bed, the boy still looked down the campfire out of the window of the shelter. The squirrel next to him confirmed that they would really take care that he could sleep peacefully at night, and that he will surely find his way to home.

In the morning the boy woke up in his hut. The squirrel was gone. The boy felt the dew of the morning on his skin and rubbed his eyes. He woke up the mind filled with peace and confidence as he looked out of the window. And what did he see? He was in the woods of rainbow. Trees had given up cloudy and decomposing colors for bright colors. There were yellow and purple trees, red and blue trees, orange and lime green trees. And these trees were talking with words you could understand.

The tree next to the shelter reached out for the boy and asked him to step forward and sit on the top of it. The purple tree stretched the boy to the orange tree. This in turn stretched him towards the red and blue tree.

The boy sang and danced in his mind as he travelled through the forest. Finally the forest ended and there was a field next to it. The last tree handed the boy to the ground. The boy saw the red home on the other side of the field and he heard as do were calling him home.

Mother might be worried about me, he thought. So the boy ran through the clayey field greeting the dog. The dog knew through gaze of the boy, what he had seen and found. But the mother did not understand. Mother was angry when the boy had been missing all night. "

The fairy flew away. An immense yearning came over me.

Yearning

I had been so focused on my work, for myself and for the searching with melancholy that I had pushed everything else outside. Or at least I thought I had. But the air was still passing through the gills as I was diving. I suddenly missed my son tremendously. I just couldn´t let the love towards him die. I felt his presense inside me continually. I also sensed that I thought of him constantly. I missed mornings the time to wake up him.

I missed the moments to cook for him. And I missed so much the times at the evenings, the times of the stories and the good night kiss. I even missed the times as he was full of anger and crossness and I had been able to press his small body against my chest to let his feelings to calm down. Water flowed like a bloody wound and I could not get up in the mornings. One-eyed followed me from the window. He was not able to decorate the smallest tomb with flowers.

>Can you see me now, my son
>as my face loses color.
>My strength flows on the top of water
>and strength of the man fractures, disappears.

>One reaches out his hand
>but no one holds on.
>So narrow is the road of the mind,
>as the carrying capacity is lost.

>Can you see me now, my son
>As you are gone so far away.
>Still comforts the love on my chest
>me now as the hope has passed away.

>One reaches out his hand
>but no one holds on.
>So narrow is the road of the mind,
>as the carrying capacity is lost.

Hear beyond the fairytales
as the days are getting colder.
Row your boat ashore
when it's time to wake up, to be forgotten.

One reaches out his hand
but no one holds on.
So narrow is the road of the mind,
as the carrying capacity is lost.

Can you see me now, my son
as fears of the nights appears.
I lose the fences of my emotions
as stars shines over the treasures.

One reaches out his hand
but no one holds on.
So narrow is the road of the mind,
as the carrying capacity is lost.

Singing horses

One day I heard a knock at the door. My little boy came in with a book under his arm. I kissed him a thousand times, and embraced him forever. My son looked me in the eyes,

"Daddy, I have missed you too and I have cried a lot. But I am here now. Dad, read to me this fairy tale." I looked at the book. It was named *Singing horses*. I took my dearest to sit on my lap and I began to read the story for him:

"One quite ordinary herdsman had a herd of singing horses. Herdsman often took his flock to the nearest meadow where the herd loved to compete with the wind. The horses spread their nostrils to enjoy the nuanced scent of the flowers and to separate the millions of uncertain odors. The horses sang beautiful melodies as their manes were dancing in the air and the hooves were beating their own rhythms on the ground. Sometimes a herdsman left the horses in the meadows over the night to enjoy each other´s company under the guardianship of the stars.

Once as the herdsman arrived to the meadow in the morning, the herd of the horses did not run towards him as they usually did. They did not sing, they were silent. The herdsman wondered that perhaps the night had been too cold and they just could not sing. But then days passed. Time just passed on and on and still the silence remained. Finally herdsman understood that the mist of the morning had wet the horses mistakenly.

But the day came as the a foal was born. It rose up onto to its frail feet and looked at the herd. Crying aloud, it was singing and begging the herd to accept it as their own. With its little nose it pushed the horses around it to get closer to each other. It touched the other´s feet and ran ahead of the flock. Singing with sadness it walked forward and the other horses followed him without even noticing they were doing so.

The herd of the singing horses came to the creek. The little foal walked to stand in the middle of the flow.. A tear fell down its cheek and landed in the water.

"A feeling" said the little foal. Suddenly each one in the herd felt it as the water flowed silently forward and touched their bodies. The foals' tear which had landed in the water created shining circles.
"Faith", said the foal. The herd raised the eyes and they saw the shining stars above them. Then they looked at the little foal who whispered for them:
"I trust you because I know you. I also feel that you know me too."
The herd of the singing horses knelt down in the creek and let the sorrow of the past go with current of the river. As they stood up again they swung their mane in the air. And then they began to sing, the most beautiful song ever. Now they were able to see and feel the story of their song."

The power of that story left me speechless. I kissed my son and told him how dear he is for me. My son smiled as he said:
"Dad I know that you know that I love you too!". Surely, I knew it. I hadn´t lost the love of my son even though I had lost so many moments to being able to be together. I valued as a treasure the time he spended with me. But for now it was time to say goodbye.

His mom, my exwife came to pick him up. I looked at her. It was only then as I saw her really:
      In the mids of thorns, along a worn path, stood a little girl. She picked up the living flower and sniffed the smell of it. She even tasted the petals of the flower. It was not bitter, and it was not sweet, but it grated on her palate. The girl spat a leaf out of her mouth. The scent of the flower did not feel any longer as more attractive. The blossom was no longer even beautiful, as one of its petals was ragged. The girl threw a flower among the thorns, and went on her way on the worn path.

I wondered what I had just seen and I was not ready to understand it completely. I went to the graveyard as my son had left. One-eyed nodded as if to say that he had eliminated the smallest grave. I nodded for the one-eyed.

The garden of One-eyed

One-eyed waited for me to give him my attention... I sat down and gave him permission.

One-eyed pulled tree roots from out of his palms and showed them to me. They looked like maple leaves rocking in the sunshine, pulled out by the roots. He wanted to free his mind to see what is the real truth, the truth that is more true than the life we can see. He was so sick of only tasting the fruits that were its own. It was paralyzed by the vulgarity of them. He desperately wanted them to be new, and was so thirsty to be reborn. But to get what he really needed would mean that parts of it´s kingdom should be rebuilt. By hard work he would need to pull out the plants and the roots which were producing such a poor rotten harvest.

He knew that he had tried to find solutions for too long, but had secured solusions for different equations. The normal way of doing things, with all his formulas, had captured too much and trappedhim in the bark layers. Age might bring some wisdom, but not the sullen character of mind. Children rejoice in learning new things, adults gets frustrated with knowing their limits of their capability to know.

All new plantings would not necessarily increase the singing trees, the laughing fruits, or the flower petals which would smooth the skin. But the prospect of even a single emotion or thought-provoking plant in the garden was worth the risk. Black tree branches with tepid fruit was simply depressing. There was nothing called a true life, other than the reflected mirror image of the fragile line on top of the ice.

At last he raised his heavy, wobbly hands towards the sky and felt how its hands had caused the hurricane. The hurricane that had spread all its' groaning, anger, requests, and dark thoughts towards the sun. Instead of a black hole, however, it was the light, which sucked it all inside then gave birth to a glittering drizzle out of faeries wings. All around us small plants stood up out of the black soil.

Crying, I watched how One-eyed was released from his pain.
Then he was gone. His teaching had been that I cannot live solely to give growth to the living crops, I can only surrender under the sky to let the rain come.

        And those hunters of ages,
        with dead wings to fly.
        They rose as rattling ghosts
        to appetize their ownership of time.

    Wind blowed and tree handed over the blossom,
    frost got to the ground and raised its' breath.
    In order to be free to hear;
    I got what the true heart sings as free.

    Fairies were sitting on moistened hair,
    Wiping sweat quietly, realizing:
"Drink the characteristics of your image from out of your palms.
    Be your own master in every moment.

    Sing it hard pressed notes,
    sprinkle it quietly to the ways of wind.
    As it is time to give away the chain you got;
Then it´s time to let the new birth for the leaves on your palms.

    You will feel the messages of your hearing,
    you can see the touch of your own heart.
    It´s yours ritght here and now.
    The moment and the life in you
    and you are free choose without the guards."

I got up trembling and went to the lake.

Birds and the fishes

I sat down by the lake. My living son was on my thoughts and the fairy tale about the singing horses. I thought about the deliverance of One-eyed. I wondered about the ports Socrates mentioned. I had not yet found the gates but I sensed that I was now on my own way.

Birds were flying in vibrating airflows, reflecting the waters' surface below. Birds waited. The fish breathed in water with their gills, some even with their skin. Some were dancing in the flowing currents, some were looking for food, shelter, or were just looking to play. Some fishes swam forward, or slept as the circumstances and the movement of the water happened to steer them.

A surge from the heights, diving. One of the fish had disappeared. This was as a reflection of human fear, to kill the feelings which could be exposed to danger. As love is denied in order not to get hurt.

This feeling was as bait for common sense, and the lack of it removed something important.

These thoughts scared me. I realized that my own inability to commit was due to the same chain of events. The painful experience of rejection had created in me some sort of unconcious protective effect: I was unable to love and be loved.

I knew that I would have to deal with this somehow. Perhaps the lake would not be the right environment. Perhaps I should go out to sea. I had heard that piranha can hunt from the air as well as from the water.

Yes, I should palpate and examine more details of my inner world. I should dive deeper and, if necessary, to create even a new source to obtain a clean and clear water.

Now I knew that my journey would not be in vain. I would not do it as a duty for society or because of others. I would do this for myself, with the knowledge of new fruits appearing and able to be shared with others. So I traveled to the sea.

Swirls in my own ocean

I hadn´t yet seen the sun in the clear sky but I felt how it burned my skin. The sun burned so much that I paradoxically started feeling cold. I got out of my rags and jumped into the sea for relief. Sea water immediately stung my dry skin and I had to get quickly to my boat. A few moments later I felt terribly bad, much worse than I had before going to the water.

So I sat down under the little shelter I had built into my boat. I decided to try not trying, seeing where I would end up if I would just let the sea to take me wherever it drifted. As the brightness faded away I noted how time floated past. The view on the sea was still the same as yesterday. It was getting cold and I felt it keenly. I dug under the covers beneath the bare sky. Most likely it would not rain because the sky was clear and the sea was calm.

One by one the stars made their own riddles. I knew that there were so many more of the stars than what I was able to see. As I saw the falling stars I understood it fully; why I had made my wishes as those little stones perished in space. Those were the times when the darkness got some light. It was as something hidden on my mind would have been found. Those were the times I remembered what was the hope as the stones in the sky guided my feelings and thoughts towards it.

I kept looking the sky and mused on its swirls and the extent of the whirls. Swirls of the black hole prevented everything from escaping out of its orbit. And still as the theory of relativity says, little particles of light might curve around its center without vanishing into it. That was as the hope which remained around my fear.

I knew my boat floated within similar swirling currents of the sea. I looked and followed as the colours of the sky blended and changed. The water played with rays of light during the cycles of night and day. As I had finally been quiet, long enough, I started to recognise the power of my feelings and thoughts. I was able to separate the temperature of the mass of water and the salinity of it. I recognised what was different compared to the peace I had felt long ago.

I had to treat the wounds which the salt water and sun had created. After getting the latest wounds I was pretty sure that I could observe the health of my skin better. Most likely I would not try to get relief from the salty water for my burning feelings.

Now I felt and knew that I could formulate even long lasting feelings and thoughts into a different shape. Only the right conditions were needed. Surely before the right timing it was nescessary to recognise where the swirls were located. But often it also required many falling stars and the determination to fly away.

After all, some twists were also needed, those would protect me. Every wounds I received taught me something. I needed the memory of experience to survive on the sea. It would be important to recognise accurately what can be changed and what should remain the same. I could understand and feel more deeply who I am outside of these physical laws. Until that time I should rely on my capability to observe myself and the reality of all life around me. I would also need to observe all the reflection which would come out of me and toward me. I should try to understand the basis of the natural laws, as much as I was able. So I could understand the parallels between the sea and the firmament.

Hamleti´s treasures

I had been three years at sea. In this salty sea, where minerals and emission floated. It all had ended here which could not stay in crystal clear streams and freshwater lakes.

I had come to this sea because I knew that I had to get to know my own sea. There was so much that human beings did not know yet: Hidden stories in the dark depths of the sea, old as milennia. There had lived the animals in the sea which had created strange forms to survive. I had built devices so that I could get deep down to retrieve those wonders and treasures. In fact, diving without a device you could reach only up to a certain point – that´s why artificial assistance was necessary.

I had colonized this island that had been desert before. Or to be honest, it had been desolate only of human beings. Plants and animal populations had lived there before me and my collection. The only observation I have seen from the rest, referring to humanity, had been long-masted wobbly things on the horizon without any real direction to go.

It was the anniversery of my departure to sea. I had been in isolation away from other people for so long that I was greatly surprised when a black vessel sailed towards my boat. Remarkably, it did not do anything to pass me. This was unusual since generally, pirates would approach perpendicular with a wooden vessel at night so that the ship cannot notice them until it is already too late. But this vessel came towards me in broad daylight and from my side. The sun was already lighting the ship from afar, with its black and multicolored flag. I waited. I did not panic, because I knew that I could do nothing else but surrender.

I was surprised as the young Danish prince Hamlet stepped out of the vessel. With firm steps he came to my boat and told me immediatly what was on his mind:
"This part of the treasures and wonders belongs to me: sadness, bitterness and revenge an the loss of everything. I choose them to belong to me from the bottom of this sea ages ago and I do not want to share them with others anymore. But I will give you this drink. After you have drunk this you will recieve sensitivity which belonged to me before."

Then Ofelia came up from the sea. Ofelia put out her hand towards Hamlet, who turned his head away, looking at his mother, who was crying at the window of his ship´s prison tower.

Ofelia implored me with this request:
"Give me everything that I am due. Give me the betrayal which is around the corner, give me the feeling of losing yourself and the feeling of losing the joy of life. In return I will give you all the love that I have ever had."

I watched how Ofelia´s words struck like swords into Hamlet. His body and whole being bled. Hamlet believed that he deserved it all. Swirls were born into the waters' surface and those reached the same droplets all over again. Ofelia sank back into the depths of the sea. Then I saw a coat rise up from the bottom of the sea. Hamlet told me that it was a gift to me from Ofelia. This garment would let my skin feel all the love and dreams Ofelia had held.

Hamlet demanded that I give to the queen her role at this play: the betrayal, the loss of joy, losing the faith in goodness, loss of ones' most deepest dream, self-hatred and self-loss.
"This reinforces the walls of her prison," said Hamlet with a smile on his face, "In return, I will give you this bag of dust, but use it skillfully and under the right conditions, otherwise lust will lead you into the same prison as my mother."

"One piece of advice I will still give to you", said Hamlet, continuing, "as you sail in these seas, as you walk in the fields and as you plant your garden, remember and be certain who is the true king. Remember the vision you had on the horizon a year ago. That small ferry made out of timber, the ferry built with a way too high of a mast. For the lust for power brings with it cold and impenetrable walls. If you choose to serve a false king, it brings the the end of life as a living soul and you have to wander as a ghost whereever you go. So only reach for what is good and reasonable.

You have now gotten to know the sea, your own sea. Your place and time has not come to be a part of the sea and of the passage of the sea. So go back to your people. Take true treasures with you as you go. Do not hide them in a coffin or put into exhibition cases, you must carry them with you. Speak about them and stand for them.

That small bag you have, hold that in a secret place. Share it only at beautiful moments when you have shared your coat as the sleeping bower in your garden for the rest of your life."

I was ready to get back to my own people. The sea was like the memory of all of humanity. The sea would also be inside of me, but now I could feel the smell of it.

> I walked on the water,
> as long as I could.
> It vibrated below my feet,
> until:
>
> The light broke its journey far and wide,
> darkness did not swallow it.
> Memories flew back as birds,
> illuminated the space behind
> that sunken sun.
>
> I felt something new,
> water got its power again.
> I just can no longer use the benefit of its surface tension.
>
> Distant solar,
> the king of heaven arc and the stars.
> Miracles are in front,
> until I dared to look at:
>
> Sea Power is deposited,
> air also fights with the line of battle
> I'm looking for here reconciliation and balance
> As the of the mirror clears.

Equivalence of time and occasions

I had met some of my fears and many deep feelings which were part of my adulthood.
I had learnt to hang wallpaper on the hard floor of my eyelids as each night came. I wanted to give up my heavy thoughts so I filled up my bed with damp moss at evening. I hung stars to shine above my bed and I said to myself: I do not have to worry. I said to myself that yes, I am known. I demanded myself to believe that here and now I own this, this nest of peace. Fog entered my rooms and I was ready to dance with the fog. The iron door had a gap that was large enough, as I slept.
During that time I didn´t yet understand that time and the occasions were not linear. Time and occasions were exponentials, logirithms, that were interlaced. I had to learn these equivalences so that I could define the logirithm. I had to understand the relation of my deep feelings and occasions and how those reflected on my reactions today. Exponents would be a key element to see and understand each feelings as it related to the current occasion and vice versa.

So how do I value the reflections of the past I meet today? That would be a clear equivalence, a logical operation, which would help me to pass the time from a different direction without being held for some undefined way of reaction.

This is the journey of my life. The roots of it does not go only to my childhood but back into the generations before me. The more I saw the relations of all things, the more I could understand causal relationships. I that way I would be free to be who I really am.

Grandpas' field

The mill

There were many different sounds near the mill. The mill itself broadcast its own voice as the millstones churned grain and the ailerons rasped above. The wind screeched through the ailerons and the birds sang nearby. Grandpa was proud of the mill he had built. Grandpa´s opinion was that grinding grain was the most thankful and merciful moment of the year.

Grandpa enjoyed the voice of the mill and the life that the mill kept alive. Grandpa sold some of the grain for the people of the village, but for the poorest of all he gave it away for free. Grandpa had a speical saying he said for these as he handed them a sack of grain. The saying was: "Remember the honest judgement: to be open and brave." This was his way of encouraging the poor to see themselves as the creation of God himself. Grandpa knew that secular property was not the dimension of humankind. Grandpa also knew that no one wanted to be poor. Diseases and deaths of the men, the breadwinners of the families, had brought a lot of poverty. During that time no one was poor because of being lazy. The least active were among those rich people who had inherited their wealth without doing anything in and of themselves. Grandpa called them spiritually poor people because often the sparkle of their clothes revealed the glassy gaze of their eyes. Of course, not all the of all the rich were spiritually poor, either.

Grandpa was a wise man. Near the mill grandpa often reminded others how important it was to use and maintain its internal machinery, otherwise the mill would fail and its' power to capture the wind to grind grain would get rusty.

Bad weather

Water ran steadily down the drainpipe. Leaves got wet and little by little decayed into black soil lumps. The mass of the leaves clogged the waterways, keeping them from running. Those leaves had been singing before, like thousands of dreams, on the trees. Now those same leaves were nauseating to look at. Grandpa came away from his field in horror:
"The entire grain harvest is lost due to the amount of this water. How can it destroy and kill this way?"
The falling rain was heavy, weary and hard. It didn't absorb into the grain softly, but crushed the grain down with all its power. The same substance, which had enabled the growth of the grain, destroyed it now.

Grandpa continued angrily: "Although the human body has water seventy per cent water and the earth has also seventy percent, must it have to rain so much all at once? And especially at this, the most critical time!"

Even the dog ran towards home, its tail between its legs. Thunder rumbled once again through the air.
 "It's probably scared," said the little boy. The boy said it so loud that grandpa did certainly hear it. But Grandpa did not say anything. He just continued worrying about his grain. The boy whispered softly into the dog's ear:
"Do not worry, I'm scared too, really. If you comfort me, I'll comfort you too. But let´s not stay in this rain. Grandpa will keep watching this rain and storm, and he will show his anger towards the master of this all, so we don´t need to do so." The boy and the dog walked inside.

Grandpa at the gates

Suddenly the rain and wind stopped. Grandpa watched it happen in the field as if it were from another dimension. A great silence fell on his ears, and his eyes ran through the years of life. All what was dear to him, and all he loved. All the major joys and sorrows. Grandpa felt down into the hay field. Just as fragile, he snapped, just as living grain stalks had broken under the rain.

Nobody could know and understand why and how. Not even what really happened. But at the same time there had been also another death. The true death. Death in a car crash, and they had rescued the one that was commanded to protect it all, the source of life itself. How and why grandpa´s life was got to be saved, no one knew.

But after the black cloaked days and too bright nights, Grandpa opened his eyes again. Something very special had happened. Grandpa recognized the melody playing on the radio. He knew all the instruments, which ones were used. He knew the tune, and it rose up from the source of life. From that foreign stranger had become part of him. And grandpa could no longer be the same. Even though every wrinkle in hands and the dry cracks on his heels showed him to be his same old self.

There lived a great secret within him, the secret that no one could understand. It was a great mystery how he could suddenly hold someone elses' memories as own.

I was grateful that grandpa did not yet leave us. I was so greatful that the rain managed to beat down only the fields. Inside of myself I also knew that grandpa was able to hear better a drop of water on his skin. He also could see now the flowing streams in my arms.

But Grandpa had not lost the sense of his own memories. Once, I heard as he told about his life to my father in cottage. I pretended that I was sleeping because I sensed that his words were meant only for my father. That night Grandpa spoke about many things that he had always kept silent.

Grandpas' Iron Youth

"I did what I was told, as a soldier must do. I did it none the less, even though I knew what I was doing was wrong. I was ordered to transport prisoners of war to Orivesi´s prison camp, camp number 23. Those who had Jewish ancestry would be later exchanged for Finns, or so I had heard.

I was forced to spend some days in a prison camp while I waited for a new assignment. In the camps, prisoners were divided according to their origins and that would effect their treatment. A lot of people died in those places, almost one-third. The Finnish Army captured more than 50,000 submitted enemy, during the Continuation War in 1941 during the attack phase. Later they would take 10,000 more.

I would have rather been fighting at the frontiers, where the enemy would remain unknown. But the rules had to be obeyed. The prison conditions were miserable.

In Orivesi´s local newspaper, I read declarations of the racial doctrine. Those were written by my comrade-in-arms, the people that I knew. Declarations made me sick. The same brothers served in a war prison camp. You were able to see and feel their thoughts through the rough touch of their hands.

Eventually, I learned to envy the dead, the soldiers of my own country, foreign enemies, or prisoners of war. As I was guarding in POW camp I learned to envy even the escapees who were shot. Their departure was faster than those who dying of disease and starvation. Deep valleys of my feelings started to depart from this life. I was able to stick to my task only because I had promised my wife that I would come back alive.

For some reason, I had to transport three Jewish children once, to be handed over to a concentration camp. One of the children was only an infant. That duty was the heaviest one for me. I would have tried to rescue them, but there were a few German soldiers watching closely over this special transport.

After the war, prison camp No. 23 was abolished. The year was 1942. My wife was expecting a child at that time. It was then that I read the news from the paper. I said nothing, because a one week trip, a holiday, followed immediatly afterwards. I felt guilty but that was no sense to refuse these momentary feelings of bright spirits. During that week I went to Jyväskylä railway. I took flowers from meadow and put them next to the railway, in memory of the prisoners who had built it. For some reason it eased the pain a bit.

The railway was the tangible memory they had left behind. And surely that memory was only the iron heart I got. About fifty Jews was eventually exhanged for Finns. I found out later the final destiny of those Jewish children: they had been shot in Tallinn.

All of this was far too much, I knew. And yet I had to continue, to move forward, and to live with this iron in my heart, because my wife would soon be a mother and the fields would not surrive without workers. So I resolved to live on, day by day. My job was to push my power into the field, so that my child would have bread to eat."

I had so far listened quietly to grandpa´s story, pretending that I was sleeping. But now I couldn't keep hiding under the blanket, because I heard grandpa crying. My father was too. I took the blanket into my arms and walked into the room.

Grandpa looked at eyes of the son,
and he saw himself.
Touched as fatherless touches
to this hair as ochre.

Hands so old have seen so much,
the lost is even greater.
The will of man has passed over,
over all the prohibitions.

But the love beats in my chest,
I have seen it all – even more!
And the son of mine
is asking forgiveness – so am I!

A field whispers the words with beauty,
the fear finally loosens its' touch.
I have been loveless:
What a lie of the lies.

The pain was too hard,
reveals the guilt deep down.
I was left all alone,
I did not dare to share.

But the love beats in my chest,
I have seen it all – even more!
And the son of mine
is asking forgiveness – so am I!

Grab into field with the brave mind,
the grain has ripened.
Let´s go from now on,
let us be true in a present time.

Give up your sorrow, open the secrets,
I am beckoning you to do so.
I did not know by then,
even though that what I wanted the most.

But the love beats in my chest,
I have seen it all – even more!
And the son of mine
is asking forgiveness – so am I!

Grandpa's death

Grandpa lived with us during the last years of his life. He was sleeping at that time on the sofa in our corridor, as he had given away all his other worldly possessions. He had already accepted the fact that he could not take away from this life any more than the soul.

As a child I often slept next to him. I felt so safe, behind his back. It was like all the evil of the world would have been far off. Grandpa would protect me from anything. On Sunday mornings when I woke up I remember he would often already be awake, listening to the Russian Orthodox church ceremony on the radio.

But one morning when I woke up, grandpa was not awake. After a while I laid behind his back, waiting, until I said "Grandpa wake up."

But he did not wake up. I tried to shake him with my small hands, but Grandpa did not stir. I got up and looked at grandpa's face and shook him even harder. Grandpa still did not wake up. I did not understand. Finally, I went to wake up my parents and told them that I could not get Grandpa to wake up. Father replied that I should let him sleep because he can be tired. I went back into Grandpas' room, and played on the floor for the moment in front of him. Finally, my father came in, with a nagging concern that I had said that Grandpa would not wake up. Father came over and saw immediately Grandpas' pale face. He touched his hand, it was cold. Grandpa had died.

The ambulance arrived. Very quickly they found that grandpa was dead. They said that we should have called a hearse instead of them, but they promised to take Grandpas' body with them. He went away and never came back. An additional period of grace had worn out.

Even then, as a child, Grandpas' death next to me was a natural thing. I was saddened that safety that I had found with Grandpa was gone, but the death itself did not seem scary. He had had a peaceful face.

Even today I remember something special I had heard at the funeral. Grandpa had asked my father to recite the words he had written in his memory:

> "What would they say,
> if they would be silent?
> Life is beautiful fragility,
> they would know it deep down.
>
> I am just a mirror, filled with cracks,
> which reflects light unevenly,
> bringing every shadow across
> by touch, gaze, in prayer.
>
> What little I know is,
> that God is great.
> His possibilies has no boundries.
> That's just what I wanted you to know,
> even after this period of time."

Later, while walking in one of Grandpas' fields, my mind always came to that moment, when I woke up behind grandpa´s back, when I could not awake him. In my thoughts Grandpa was still reaping hay in his fields. It was Grandpas' field, because he was a part of that field.

Grandfather's wish was that his body would be burned and the ashes scattered by the wind over his farm. "The Earth is where I will return," he had said.

Child in me

The Ruined fence and the falling star

I had been sitting on this fence before. I had watched the airplanes while sitting here.

Every now and then amateur pilots had risen into the air. They had wobbled from side to side as they asked the most from the carrying capacity of air. Now I wondered if the fence could support me anymore.

The night was already darkening. The cold, moist breath of the evening stroked my cheeks as I looked up at the sky. Stars and planets greeted me quietly. Or at least it seemed to me that everything was as it was before.

But then it happened, something surprising. Simultaneously with a shooting star, I rose upwards into the air. I had decided that life had to be found elsewhere. How could it be that all my spirituality, symbolized by the stars, would have only an empty and rumbling significance?

There had to be life. I dove to Jupiter first. I watched masses of particles, the size of dust, and then moved moungain-sized chunks of rocks away, in front of them. I bent down to admire the moon: the surface had a geyser plunging the fluid out into space. I smelt the volcanic fumes rising from the top of another moon and I picked up ice from the surface of a third, finding organics and fluid water, hydrogen and carbon. I found the seas inside of the planets. But I did not find life. I could not find life even occurring in another state of being. It was certain that I did not find anything that you could name as growth, feeling, thinking or love. It made me tremendously angry.

I threw planets and moons out of my hands. I took support once again from the fence. It wobbled under my hands. Perhaps its life expectancy had reached its peak. Soon it crashed to pieces under me. Would the same thing happen to the Earth?

I got up and walked to my childhood home. Everything looked suddenly old, and primitive.

The mill was deteriorated. I said aloud that not even Grandpa or Socrates would like what I saw! I smirked. Now the Home of my childhood was empty, uninhabited. However, the timbers breathed just as well now as they had in the past. I walked into the room, where a rocking chair quietly waited for someone to be seated. The baking oven was waiting someone to get it warm. I waited for my memories to come from my childhood.

I opened a wooden trunk quietly. There was a lot of papers and a few black and white photographs. From the top of all, I found a poem, which exuded through its words what kind of devotion, reverence and fear with which it was written. It was written by my grandfather:

"Finland, my country.
My country with the blood of my brothers,
the valleys of peace.
We fought there,
quietly on the trenches,
against the enemy at war,
looked at the future without fear.

I wanted to give it as an inheritance
for the daughters and sons of this country.
You unknown brother of me,
did the same alongside.
You were in front of me as the barrier,
when a bullet of the enemy
pierced you.

Did your children know,
how great was the sacrifice,
how did the brave men run.
My country, my own,
dust of it was hidden from you.

You were left behind, somewhere in there,
cross remained and the memories.
Part of myself stayed there too,
I got the memories so heavy on my chest.

Our country, country where I was born.
Land of our fathers and the wars of them,
Did you forget your fatherland?
Were in too rush to get allied,
braking the power decision-making of own.

Does it shackle itself,
just to hang gold necklaces?
Does it transfer itself,
torn in half between the richest and the needy?

Where is the courage
wars with words and deeds for freedom,
on behalf of the land,
that was released by your prayers and sacrifices?

My country, my country where I was born,
There were too many left behind,
expensive price was paid.
By what justice,
now bread crumbs are handed out to the winds of the heavens,
carrion birds to eat the children's bread.

Finland, my country.
My land of the blood of my brothers,
the valleys of peace.
We fight yet,
hands across at the morning and evening?

Brothers and sisters of my brothers.
Do we remember yet,
or did we forget the deaths too soon?
Did we forget,
what is to have land under you fingers?
What is the whispering of the winds, singing under the spruces?

What is burnt fields and frosty years?
What is a shortage, when all exported?
What is the pain brought in mourning?
Do we forget the blessing of the Lord?
Do we see as contemptible a gift given?"

My grandfather had always been very patriotic and religious. But he was right, it was more difficult to appreciate freedom before you realize the loss that is neccesary before gaining it. Grandpa had tried to give me and my father his enduring truths, but in fact I had stored them in my own attic.

Fishes underneath

I looked thoughtfully through the black and white photographs I had found. I found a picture of me standing beside my father and grandpa, and each of us holding up all the fish we had caught. I was clearly the proudest one of my catch, even though as the smallest man I also had the smallest fish.

I remember vividly as I was growing up, becoming interested in fishing. I was attracted by the fact that I was able to guess, by the location and time, what fishes I could catch. In addition, the movements of the fish on the line and strength of its pulling helped me to accurately guess what size it was. It was like validating your own feelings as I wondered what kind of fish I had caught with which lure.

The nearby lake became a familiar and safe place where my mind could be calm. Being alone wasn't a problem , even if I didn't catch anything. The tension of whether or not I would catch anything, was sufficient. My mind got to wander while I fished, and time lost its meaning. The only that mattered was this moment and the possibility of a catch.

The surface of the water shimmered, something had gone to catch the bait. However, I did not manage to set the hook in time. The disturbance of the fish was like a peaceful breeze on my spiritual landscape, which continued its free course. However, my alertness increased after each attempted strike and I was more ready to set the hook. In my mind I speculated what type of fish it was. It had to be pike this time, because of the strength with which it pulled. But the pike was teasing me this time, and I hardly got the chance to reel it in.

Rarer fish were the most interesting. These I kept and brought home to be smoked. I wanted to taste a bit of those myself too. I kept the pike only it they were really big, otherwise I let them go. Certainly, a pike was a good catch, but not so special as to celebrate.

Several summers I spent by the lake. By then I had grown to be a man almost without noticing it. But even grown, my mind always sought its way back there. In winter, I fished through the ice, in summer by boat and from the shores.
As the lake began to freeze each fall, the four degree water of the lake sank to the bottom as the surface became colder. The water itself protected the fish, kept them alive through the cold winter. The water on the surface froze over and was able to carry even strong men on its skin. I knew the fish on my lake, no one questioned that. While I was there no one demanded anything. There was only the small hopeful anticipation of the catch and an abundance of peace, even though I of would carry nothing away from its shores.

I looked at the photographs, smirked, then felt myself grow melancholic. I was reminded of some unpleasant memories, as well. It had been always hard for me to apologize, even as a child. Deep down I always wanted to do the right thing and therefore it was very difficult to admit that I had sometimes done something wrong. It reminded me of the time that my father had forbidden me to go for rapids alone, without an adult´s supervision. But the boy next door had asked me to go with him, and I went. My father was furious, at both of us.

It took me a long time to admit that my father by no means meant that the younger son of a neighbors' would be enough to accompany to go to the rapids. It took a long time to admit that the little punishment I got, not getting icecream for a month, was deserved. In the end, with tears in my eyes, I asked for forgiveness from my father. And he forgave me. How reassuring it was to know that my father loved me, even though I had done a wrong thing.

Now I had to admit to myself that I would have to ask forgivenes from loved ones and some others, but also, from myself.

Dragonfly

There it sat, looking at me with big green eyes. It was prepared for our meeting better than I was. It had lived a long period in its larval stage underwater, and had survived. It had had the courage to hatch out and leave the security of the water, and it knew how to fly.

It was not afraid. It grabbed my arm harder with its sucker-legs. Its wings were still proudly outstretched. It would live for only a day, so long of a moment for it, but still, it looked at me.

I spoke to it. At first I just said, "Hey, what's up?" But, no, it was not even created with eyeflashes to be able to wink back. "You're not afraid of me?"
It corrected the position of the feet and hold me more firmly.
"You're just checking me out," I chuckled. I drank a bit more coffee. I turned my head away. Then it took off, its wings making a helicopter-like sound. My eyes followed it until it had flown to the flowers and then farther away up to the slopes.

In the life between the two miles,
I can jump around them.
I can crash by design,
accidentally sometimes,
I admit it.
But it is the child in me,
who, laughing and playing.

And I sing this song:
ae ae ae aee.
And I will make reconciliation with myself.
I do not deny anything anymore:
ae ae ae aee.
The life I have lived.

Safe under the blanket, familiar,
I curl, double up.
I play with the pictures of my dreams,
and I fall asleep.
The world fresh, new,
it opens the secrets of itself,
I am not afraid of the dark.

At the grandpa´s field, I see everything,
in the rhythm of each step.
Yesterday is in me,
even in grandpa´s wrinkles:
you are smiling.
Do not regret me anymore,
I am in you.

And I sing this song:
ae ae ae aee.
And I will make reconciliation with myself.
I do not deny anything anymore:
ae ae ae aee.
The life I have lived.

And I paint this memory:
ae ae ae aee.
And I will make the moment to look like us.
There is still time left:
ae ae ae aee.
In this moment is the life.

And I sing this song:
ae ae ae aee.
And I will make reconciliation with myself.
I do not deny anything anymore:
ae ae ae aee.
The life I have lived.

And I paint this memory:
ae ae ae aee.
And I will make the moment to look like us.
There is still time left:
ae ae ae aee.
In this moment is life. Right now.

I tied my shoelaces, in order to travel, at last, to the gates. I cleaned my glasses to be able to see anything oncoming and also, to see myself. I stood up straight and tall; my own value as a human had returned. One heart and one mind within multicored time, I thought. So it must be!

The son

Water will bear

My son came to visit. This time he came to live with me. He asked me about my travels and I told him with excitement about what I had learnt:

"Water will bear. It really will bear but the wind will carry you forward and the driving sails give the direction where to go. Using the sails requires a great deal of skill. But you could do nothing with them and all of your skills, without the wind. If you go further out on the sea, you will have to learn to read your position from the stars. Because sometimes everything else can disappear from the horizon. Worst of all is when the clouds are covering the stars. Black, dark and cold nights are much better than mild and cloudy weather. It is really rare that anyone wants to be lost at sea for a long time."

"What do you do then, if you run out of the drinking water?" Asked the boy.

I replied to him:
"Salt water can be made drinkable, by distillation. But you can't drink it otherwise."

"Why is sea water salty?" Asked the boy.

I continued:
"Because the water takes minerals from the ground as it continues the journey from upriver. Along little creeks, rivers, and rapids, water will flow into the sea. Water is no longer running out from the sea. Surface of the sea water can evaporate when it´s a hot day, of course, but it would no longer flow. For this reason, minerals, including salt, will remain in water and therefore it is salty, contrary to the lake water. The lake is only a transit point for water. The sea is a destination."

Small droplets began to fall from the sky, freckling the surface of the water. Clouds had come from the ways of the winds, heavy with water vapor. The droplets rebounded into the air from the water surface as if they were bouncing on trampoline. It was music, and dance.

But one drop was not ready yet, to fall and did not want that surrender, to be owned by the sea. It experimented with surface of the sea allowing the water to flexed beneath it but notlet itself fuse. The sea understood, and gave it time, watching peacefully as it palpated the other drumming drops. But at last the drop allowed itself to be blended into the water mass and was as one with the sea.

Now it was raining really hard!

My son and I laughed together, soaking wet in the rain and we decided that since we were wet already, so we might as well go for a swim.

As I was swimming, joy flowed in my ears from the surface of the water and created new growth for the dry garden within. Time ran in my fingers, causing a smile to come over my hands and body. I drunked my head beneath the surface and I felt as if I were being born again. I felt my thoughts in a new way and at the same time as if I'd forgotten.

My sons' bluish lips had disappeared, and he shouted happily, "See, now I know how to swim! Father see!" Along the water echoed as the choral singing towards the air and shores," I know how to swim, swim, swim!"
I joined with the echo, and I felt, how my clapping hands underwater transformed into fins and my feet transformed into a fishtail. I dove without drowning, I smiled. I could be myself and swim in my sea. Because the water is a part of me and I belonged to part of it too.

Finally, it was time to get out of the sea and go back to the land. We washed the seawater from our skins and warmed up in the sauna. Then I put my son to bed, covering him up to sleep.

I was so proud of him. And I was so very sorry that I had been so long in the travels of my own mind. The next night I slept very peacefully.

A Funny Dream about the Royal Family

As I slept I was free to see what so ever to happen. My imagination did not have rules to follow any of my thoughts and feelings in a dream. My thoughts did not have the same logical way as during the light of the day. I was just drifting on.

As I slept I dreamt about a fairy tale and the drama that ensued. Some famous king was dead and I was exploring the castle. The prince told me about the events that had transpired but somehow he looked just like a boy from my childhood. We looked through some photos together.

The king had come from abroad and had been married to a Finnish artist-designer, whose grief came out as anger. Some of queen´s youngest relatives, who also lived in the castle, had got used to the Queens' continual fury over everything, but eventually they did not bother to care about her.

Now Queen got angry when someone asked her, how one scarf is made of and what is the recipe for "holes in the fabric paper".The Queen shouted and banged the doors. Such scarves were for sale and on a studio next to the memorial table. As the queen's brother came to the scene he said that do not worry, she will calm down. "Let's ask about it from the cantor, she probably knows the answer, as the cantor remembers almost everything." We walked down to the hall, where she was dressed in orange scarf.

Cantor was a bit sturdy and she was just explaining excitedly to cantor student': "Oh Can I go to register A Gipsy´s celebration on. Could you work as a cantor here on saturday? We have been seeing each other and made some plans!". The cantor made patterns in the air with her orange scarf and smiled widely. "Now there is an event and man´s family is invited and there is going to be great serving. Well, who knows, maybe it´s going to turn out to be wedding." Again cantor did patterns in the air with the scarf and took some dance steps.

The Queen's brother began to laugh, he was always in a good mood. He began to tell the story by singing, "That would be somethin indeed! For I also have booked a meeting and I need help from my daughters for that..."

As he sang he streched his voice: "Ooodette and Aaadanne", my daughters, I need your help. " Little girls looked questioningly at his father. "Yes, your father is going to get married. And this wedding will be a spectacle."

Queen´s brother continued with monotone voice, "So what should we act on this play?, It goes like this..." The Queen's brother and the son of the court presented now, how you should lay down your shoulders. After this, they raised their hands just above the breast wrists relaxed. They were acting as panting dogs. "So who are we, what shall your roles be at the play?", sang the Queen´s brother. His daughters showed with the head movements, they do not know. Then he changed his face expression to be as a sad laugh and sang: "Well, after all, it is difficult to play the role of a messy Saturday morning!"

I woke up for my own laugh. Laughter and hope had made space in me. I knew know that it is just fine to not understand everything within me. I also had felt how the free soul can create new things to appear on the scene.

At the gate

Without noticing as if secretly,
I looked at the furrows on my hands.
There was no longer silence of the morning,
not the dive of the night.

I saw so much more,
more than my fallen dreams.
I saw the man,
whose heart beats in my chest.

Without noticing, as if secretly,
the feeling wrapped to the thought.
Blew softly the words eternal,
death is present.

But your memories whispers,
child unanswered, asks.
Iron armor goes green,
as your heart beats the rhythm.

Without noticing, as if secretly
dewdrops flow.
Meet the furrows, confers rest,
morning beats the night.

I saw so much more,
more than deepening furrows.
I saw its reflection,
for which my soul has been created.

At last he had arrived on the gate of the souls altar, where his ego was created and born. He watched rapturously nudity where the reflections of godliness were drawn to humanity. The persona drew the contours of feelings and experience of being. That mysterious source, where the words of different languages mixed to be a marvelous internal tune, bringing messages of right and wrong, speaking about this time, and the afterlife to come. The garden where children are playing around with curiosity and freedom to think, to question and to learn.

The garden, which has not been been built on dead trees, but where all the trees are living and healthy.

Each trees' seed has become windblown, who from afar, who closer. Some of the seeds has traveled inside a bird in a shelter of wind and air currents. Some of these wind has caught with its power of ideas and intellect. But all these seeds are gathered here at the gate of the souls altar, to grow in all vulnerability. Some, however, arrive just before the last evening rays of light reflects on the surface of the water.

>Morning arrived,
>doubled up the night.
>Cabinets of it remained empty.
>Light brushed
>the hair of the trees,
>it calmed the roads of the wind.
>
>Spells on the skin
>spilled over,
>covered the wrinkles,
>time, and ideas
>and beyond.
>
>Deer stretched out their heads,
>turned their ears to hear:
>but they do not,
>only the silence.
>
>Flowering spikes
>and ochre
>are a robe on the land.
>Yes, they feel, they know the step.
>They feel the birds as wreaths
>and the midnight sun over their shoulders.
>The morning haze,
>is only one breath of the sigh.

A man of his time in space

Someone has theorized that water could be present outside of the space we comprehend. This would be quite logical. After all, a human being has the skin and the tactile senses. We as people are held together, balanced with emotions. The human subconscious is like unexplored space. The Creator himself shows the power of creativity within the stars in the sky and also by creation of mankind as His own image. However, we actually know so little, and only of this physical reality, and not well even that. We monitor our physical body functions and our symptoms, so much more than the person as a whole. So much more gorgeous, more complex, more valuable is the worth of a human being.

If you look at only the physical characteristics and the economic value of man, human being is not worth very much in monetary terms. The value of the chemical components of man is about one euro; five euros if you add the value of our skin. If you look at human efficiency, what a man can achieve, his value is much higher. When we consider the value of a person for their loved ones after being murdered, their value might be just 10 000 euros. Still, none of these prices will ever replace the loss of a loved one.

I had lost great deal after all. I had felt that the divorce was the only right solution at the time. I was tired of living my life in my own body and that is why it had been so hard to be close to others. I did not know myself at the time, and I didn't have my dignity. That's why I did not understand the value of other person either.

I was so blessed that I had met Socrates.

I was relieved that the skeletons were named and buried. I was relieved that the animals of my subconscious had been encountered. Meeting Hamlet was also a significant turning point in the journey, because in the end it is the fresh water that keeps the man alive.

My sweet water was that beautiful woman that I had rejected. I had abandoned her before her actions. She had probably forgotten me already. But can the same tree ever forget itself?

If the wind has once sang on the branches, if the lyrics are written on the leaves of emotions' scent, can you even breathe without knowing that reality? It may well have been that I had wrongly interpreted the songs of the birds, but I did not want any longer to miss even a single moment of those times.

I started to run towards the bridge. The bridge would surely be repaired -or we could rebuild it. At least I could build my side as far as possible. It shall be an arch that meets in the center!

WOMANS' GETAWAY

Blood runs in a goblet

It melted the cold
and poured out.
Time ran on the ways of the swamp,
and knelt wounded.
We drank blood, drank from goblets,
washed our eyes with salt
to hear the buried messages.

The son of eagle carried a cat,
taught it to fly with its wings.
Shot artists with an arrow.
Speak quietly away the headaches.

Paleness in the cheeks reveals all!

Runs through the forest,
deer is wounded.

But still, it runs.

Discovering the scene of legitimate murder

My forehead was active, my thoughts wandering but fixing themselves on nothing. I was afraid of these moments, unconsciously and consciously. It was safer to focus on washing, cleaning, washing ...

Then all at once it came to my mind: the image of the crimp of four fingers and the curve of the little finger, a small crinkly ear and a wider neck. The nurse looked at me seriously, and said, with certainty: "You should do an abortion as soon as possible." This was also what the doctor had confirmed.

My husband disagreed, but I felt he did not understood the responsibility that would arise if I would have given permission for this child to see daylight. Now, however, I understood it all. I had murdered part of myself at that time. The guilt was tremendous. What if the diagnosis had been wrong? And even if it had been correct, so what?

Who would I be without this guilt, without the guilt that came suddenly around the corner in these moments? I had managed to run away fairly effectively without facing the issue. Fortunately, only a few people knew about the pregnancy, and those who knew had encouraged me to stick with the decision. There were other considerations, as well. Of course it was important that both of us were able to work. It was important to get our loans paid off. All these things, after all, were important ... but in the end, after everything, they were not.

However, I could not undo anything. I could never completely bury that little child of mine, that part of myself that was also part of my husband. But I had buried a lot in our relationship, because I was the one that had had to ultimately make that decision.

For years I had been looking for mercy by punishing myself. I had left my husband, because I believed that for him it was better to be without me, to be free of the evil person I had become.

I had even cheated on him so that it would be easier to hate me. I had demanded that our son lived solely with me. But as our son grew up, he was able to express his own will.

I never could redeem myself. I would have to find my way back to my child so that I could be forgiven. Everything else, all those things that had once been so important, had lost their meaning, because I had lost everything. Only my broken self was left. Only real pure water could heal these shattered and worn, parts of me.

Pain

It circled and curved around my head, until it decided to make a nest in my hair. I carried it around on my head, until it decided to dig in, nesting deeper into me. It devoured my hair and finally sidled into my brainstem, deep into my neck, sending out its horrifying melody along my nervous system.

Suddenly I saw small balls of light and smelled the scent of coffee, and burning. Unreality seemed to be true and I felt as dizzy as a slave after days on a stormy sea. I was groping my way in the dark and I tried to find a word from the branches. But the words were silent, and no one understood what was wrong with me.

But all of this was from this unknown creature. All marveled at its empty nest and its tiny hole in the middle of the nest. From where it had entered it had moved to sleep on the other side of my atlas vertebra. It had pushed my neck, twisting it, and was not hurrying to get out.

I ran from doctor to doctor, for blood tests, to the physiotherapist, to x-rays. And once again I ran. All my thoughts and my feelings began to revolve solely around my body and I realized for the first time how ones' soul resides in it. My body was in pain; my soul was the same. I was so tired and restless.

The world shook and staggered around me and I felt that trees and branches were reachng up from underfoot. The wind passed over me from afar, and the pain tightened its grip. I missed freedom. I sometimes even longed for death. To say this out loud my longing eased, although after saying it I had to explain that I would not truly kill myself. And yet life went on. I had to get used to living as broken. I had to live in the continual company of pain and judgment.

Behind the bars

I was looking at myself thoughtfully behind bars. I wondered how I had managed to build this prison. The sentence comes with punishment, I clearly understood, but what were my offences? For what was I guilty? What were these things that I and I alone was guilty of?

Of a failed marriage, for one. But I had at least gotten a reduced sentence for being married for the first time. For this sentence I had received invisible guards behind my back who continually whispered about all my failures and the impossibility of true love.

Ending up in prison was a hard fact. All my creativity and freedom was limited now. There was no room to maneuver in this cramped space. Sometimes at night the lights shouted: "Wake, wake up, to get your every days' judgement and live happily ever after!" The food had lost its flavor but the fragrances that floating behind the bars brought back strong emotional memories.

I guess I was provoked, by the guards, to commit murder. I had murdered hope. I had murdered dreams. In order not to have to repent. Now, however, while sitting in my cell, there was nothing else to regret. I had beaten myself and the love in me and I had left it all to creep. I had denied all the opportunities to live and breathe with its lungs. I was under sentence of death.

I saw so clearly outside of the bars. Being the toughest judge on myself, I wondered, what would the law of my kingdom say about act of grace? What would be the response of others? Does a new opportunity always exist, if you just embrace it?

Breaking the bars of my mind and the walls of my emotions would be a way of escape from all this. I had seen it to happen, in others. But do I want to jump down into the sea that was waiting for me, behind these bars? Would I have enough strenght to swim safely to the beach, arriving to islands, one at a time?

I knew the answers that were lurking behind the bars. I fell asleep repeating it.

The forest

In my dream I had reached the forest. I saw and heard things that I had not wanted to believe. I heard the trees mentioning the names, the names I had crucified in my mind. Flowers on the trees brought recollections of dreams to my nose. There were colorful animals and black animals. There were blind, multi-head monsters which were weeping bitterly. The roots of the trees loosened from the ground to choke me as I passed, like a group of snakes. There were angry rocks on the path which jumped on my toes. I walked forward within ecstasy and despair. I feared and loved at the same time. I was brave enough to dare to be afraid.

I was able to touch everything with my gaze. I was able to hear all that I had seen. And finally I understood so much more. Some things became clear and writ large. For the first time I understood why the fire-breathing cat, who had been lost in the wood, was trying to melt the frozen lily flowers on its paws.

The path in the forest came to a crossroad. To make a choice seemed impossible. How would I know which path should I choose? Could I turn back? I remembered how, when I was a child, I had imagined myself as a machine of dreams, able to control them.
There were different phantasms and I was able to roll them backward and forwards in time to see the beginnings of the dreams. If it started to look like nightmare or I didn´t like the look of it, I was able to go back and select a new one.

In general, I chose pleasant dreams. But sometimes, a image of the safe-looking yard turned out to be nightmare. I'd dreamt that the war had snuck up into the yard around my home, and only a bush uncovered me in a dream. But the next night I turned that dream to be a pleasant one and I made a firm decision that no war could ever proceed closer to the house than that bush. Could I, just like in these childhood dreams, therefore return back onto this once traveled path?

I sat down next to the crossroad. I did not dare to make a choice. I was used to putting salt even onto those wounds which could sprout new growth. So I waited for one of the paths would grow up and select itself. I waited for the forest to simply disappear. I waited that I would walk unconsciously two paths at the same time. No. I just waited, not even knowing what I was waiting.

Wise men of the time

There is time 'til morning
for the rulers of the night to pass.
They are arriving with the ships,
Touching on your forehead.
They draw to the air
clouds without the words.
Flame on the waters' surface,
it is possible sometimes.
A timeless moment of the human mind;
the smell of a field of barley
and the whisper of the sun on the skin.

It is a land of slaves to rise,
leave the form of their conscription.
Draw constructs on the water,
touches forgotten by hands.

The grass is growing,
and it is going to get cut.
The grass is growing,
wreaths braided.
Winter is just the moment.
The night without light.

There is time till morning,
to take the sky as a cloak to the shoulders.

Water dances with air
and the other way round.
Over and over again it flows to me,
wets my toes in secret.

During the hours of the night the water rose and covered the room completely. My bed stayed in place but I was raised into the air inside the water. Three persons were there, observing. They discussed with me: yesterday, today, and who I really am. We sat by a campfire in the woods. Gently we raised our eyes, and all of us faced each other, genuinely.

Desires and fears started the battle with their swords. They struck the sword through each others' heart, eyes, and slapped the lips from each other. But none of the three were able to proclaim the winner.

Masculinity was reflected in each of their faces, femininity came through their skin. Three weak and needy women were performing a dance for us. We remained quiet.

Water began to flow around me, it came from within the three of us, through our ears, and then ran out of sight. The middle of them finally asked: "That's what I heard and felt, is that why I came to you?"

An echo replied from the trees of the forest. Thousands of leaves sang: "Am I, whom I was appointed to be, is that the song we sing on your branches?"

The fire trembled uncomfortably. It formed the face who cried out all my names. The first nodded silently. Water danced with the air and the other way round, around us.

Then the sky was filled with the stars. They flew through the night like thousands of wishes. They gave me a new birth, quietly, in the middle of my garden. I would plant here the sources of flowers and the sky would water them.

I woke up, and the nightmares were gone. I knew who now would be in charge. But before that I had to go through it all.

The ways of the fire

The fire began to burn on the skin of my hands. I felt the warmth, but not the heat. I watched the beauty of the fire as it was eating the top of my skin and afterwards gave it up to the air to be carried far away. I did not know where it would be heading. The fire, however, was not able to burn my skin deeper, even though the flames were growing fierce.

I bent down to look at my reflection in the surface of a stream of water. I saw how the fire had spread to my guts and how it pushed flames around the sockets of my eyes for lightening the darkness. My eyebrows and eyelashes were burned away. I breathed fire, but it did not hurt. It was like an inevitable presence of form, in this moment.

The fire had burned all the hair off my head. I looked at this fact thoughtfully. I touched the skin on my skull, but deeper than that the fire had not burnt anything. It was a special fire that took everything away what I would not need, and took them, as ashes, somewhere into oblivion.

I palpated with my fingertips with a totally new way. Fully customized fingerprints submitted questions. The wrinkles of my toes were remembering the stories of the passed times. I went back inside. I heard how the clock repeated itself with the peace of rhythms. In the end, my house caught fire on contact with the force of me. That was the sign to go back to the creek and pick up what belonged to me from the will-o´-the wisp.

A cooling air

The songs of the wind subsided, but the waves still whispered the chords. My toes were in the water, but the sun had gone into the clouds. Chills crept secretly over my being, and I realized that I was completely alone.

I traced the outlines of my face with my fingers, just to see what the touch felt like. As long as I did not weep, I did not mourn. But sadness had landed on my shoulders, like a gray mist, like water releasing its heat to the air.

I walked into the water, until the mid-thigh. It was as far as I dared at this point. The water stung; it felt like millions of diamonds were instantly created on the heavenly arc of my skin. The stars were not lost, even though I did not see them at that time. The bottom of the lake gave in with my steps, and my imagination saw fish and snakes in the rocks and sticks below.

The wind brought a gentle rain. The droplets were bouncing off the surface of the water and I watched their dance. Then the creek began to speak to me:

"Do you have the ability to face your feelings? Or will your thoughts end up always behind glass, trapped behind a dirty partition, which you can see only small parts of your capacity feeling, what your thoughts are seeking? Your thought are connected to your feelings and so should your feelings should be connected to your thoughts.

One-sided communication between them leads to an ambivalent state, because the human ego exists in different dimensions of the time. As a whole human being we are truly presented with the treasures of this moment, being able to share humanity, life and the gifts of the nature.

God certainly is not limited, ever, but He is able to face even when a person is affiliated to something just as she is escaping. As she is losing the image of God from herself, and as she is bound to false selves that others have created.

Do you have time to just be and talk with yourself? Do you have the will to find the ability to have conversation and truly enter into the encounter? Do you have the will to believe and trust that you will find what you are looking for, or by grace that you will receive something that you cannot earn?

Do you have the humility to again be like a child? Do you want to be that person, for which you have been created? Do you have confidence in the Holy which you have been given as a gift? "

I stood up. And I continued my journey. I knew that I must now dare to go into the field of thistles. I would go there, even though I knew there would be packs of wolves ready and waiting for me.

The heritage

Quietly, and all the time more silently,
the contours of the walls are drawn on the horizon
and they will vanish away.
I step in the blank timelessness,
where all the hinges are removed
-or maybe they never existed.

I feel the cursed scents of transcendence,
poisoning commandments and judgment.
Truer is it the truth, than what an eye can see.

Intertwined with the discussions,
father and daughter: Answers and questions
great thoughts about human value.

Quietly, and all the time more silently,
crackly recollections.
It was not so.
You cursed in me the memories so deep!

Father

Something like that can not happen. At least no one can believe that something like that really happens. At least not that the father of a child can do it. And I had not dared to talk about it. It did not happen only once or twice, but so often that the field of thistle was raped at the same time.

The human mind, that midden of sickness and filth. A completely incomprehensible act and guarded, touched by fear that others could know. Soiled little butt, and the sky above looking on quietly. Hands too strong and commanding. In his eyes the devil himself.

Did anyone really know? Did my mother only turn away her blind, or did she not see? That woman, who herself received so many beatings by his fists. I must have the Devil's stamp on the forehead, cursed the human child. Oh, if I had not been born! Did anyone ever know what this was, this cruelty under their eyes?

You left me this heritage, you tattooed it on my skin with sorrow and fear. You did not ever say why. You just said that you could not resist.

> Thoughts will crack
> even the strongest tower.
> When the walls of the palace
> are covered with sewage.
> Death-smell flows in the corridors
> and the scents of the memory of the unclean:
>
> Hand touched the innocent.
> Penetrated inside
> to the carefully guarded place.
> Childhood was stolen
> by the sick mind of another.
> Dressed her
> with great brutality.
>
> The mind so sensitive
> was chained with fear.
> The ego was pushed away.
> The desires and passions
> unleashed the devil.
>
> In the rhythm of evil
> too much, too early, from too too many directions.
> She learned to take her first steps.

Waterlily

She stretched out her hand towards God, such as a water lily raises its stalk through the water.

She opened toward the mourning, that lived under the fear, she opened her longing, she opened all along the surface of the water. Mist and vapor rose towards the sky, whispering quietly, and crying out loud. Waterlilies were guarded at night and day. The rain watered the flower petals and water became a part of the surface, which supported it.

She saw that her toes had come through her socks` and she bent her toes, curled herself into the fetal position.

She woke up in the morning to listen to the singing of birds without getting the messages. Heathers grew attached to her skin and turned red before the winter.

She walked to the balcony to blow soap bubbles to greet the cold and felt the cold metal tingleling her fingertips. She blew harder, filling the sky with long stalks of waterlilies.

Wolves

Wolves stopped their dance. I sat silently. The leaves fell silently from the trees, humming songs old as millennia. I shivered so hard that it burned my skin. Silent hymns had arrived in this funeral. Loss, giving up, exhaustion, forfeiture. Grief.

I sat quietly watching the funeral procession. Fairies covered their faces in white robes and their staffs struck lightning towards the heavens. I watched in silence the anger that passed their sorrow. All those mothers who had lost their children, all fathers, whose children had been torn from them. All the children themselves, from whom childhood had been denied.

In the middle of the meadow ran back and forth in a raging bull. Black smoke rose from its nostrils when it cursed all its fears to the air. It ran inside an invisible cage without being able to more than bluster. In fact, it was the enemy of itself. Prisoner of the past.

Funeral procession did not care to pay attention. They were heading towards the mountains, down which slopes flowed the groans of the years and prayers of the drowned. They climbed from the mountain to the other, to mark their passage there. They left a pile of stones there to show that they had tried on.

Stone stole a wolf's face as its own. But the snow finally covered those faces -or at least so I think.

Farewell

Goodbye

I didn´t recieve love in my childhood from the parents. I had tried to live with it but I never had been able to grieve. Perhaps the after mourning it would finally release me from its grip. Perhaps only then I could receive love and could love myself. My memories asked me, demanding an answer:

"Do you have time to organize a funeral? Do you have time to say goodbye for what you never had? Did you ever drink the tea, which gave you the fragrance already on your lips? Do you miss your phantasms, which are possible, but that you have attached to the wrong wall?"

I finally decided to clean up my home. I placed paintings on the walls again. From one wall, I removed the wallpaper. To my surprise, I noticed the wallpaper was affixed with goo. It was a beautiful pattern, but was torn into tatters: it would be nicer for new tenant to move to the apartment if it were gone.

Ants were eroding routes to the floor and next to the walls. As winter turned into spring, they walked bravely into the open, as if to check if they could take over the space as their own. Each time they tried I had to poison them. Sometimes they came again and again in the spring. Sometimes, even in the summer. I had to stubbornly to start to poison them, otherwise my food would be in danger.

Traces of life appeared in my house, in spite of all rehabilitation. And the ants came along their routes. It was part of this life. Even though, I would light a candle in the evening. This last supper, after which I would be willing to say goodbye. I would make my cup of tea in peace, I would smell and taste it on my lips. I would take my cup of tea in peace and let the fire consume the wax candle. Evenings were already as bright as the mornings. And the light played beautifully with new wallpapers. I met the ants, and then I said goodbye to them. I knew I would always do what was necessary.

Funeral

I had to admit that I had been abandoned and forsaken, and that I had also missed out on a lot. My sister had died of polio as a child. My grandmother had died when I was young. I had an unborn child. My husband and son were still alive, even though I had tried to bury them in my mind. Now it was time for my mothers´s funeral. Death, death, death. The acual and forced death. The real and unintended death. So real and inevitable.

It was the grain,
which gave in so quietly.
Tears secretly on cheekbones.
It was a cessation
of song of the hearts.

What I touched,
that´s what I felt inside me.
The memories so strong and mighty!
Too many
at the gate of departure.

I asked,
at last silently.
Without the strength to wait for an answer:
when there is no more
than timeless time.

You look at me,
I know it well.
Through me, through the pain.
I am at the gates of
Death again.

Farewell,
I will leave for my beloved.
Pain slashes and commands me now.

Be near me,
hold me now.

What is the way
of man down here?
When ends the death which is near?
And the life
imperishable.

Still, I want to appreciate,
what I have been given.
It is all greater than grief!
I bless the memory
until you are found again.

So long!

There are all the ingredients for a disaster when all the waste of undealt with feelings and thoughts of experiences ends up into the subconscious. Those feelings and thoughts which are unexploited, untreated and non-formulated. Even the destruction of human life may be waiting behind the corner. All of this was like plastic, which passes unchanged through sewers into the sea. Wind, heat and tide carries the waste so easily into the medium of the ocean. Eventually, the waste accumulates mysteriosly from this offing of the ocean to all the islands and beaches of the world.

My husband had been my island and its waste area of lava-beach. I had started to bury alive the environment with my own plastic waste without paying attenstion to what I was doing. I should cleanse the plastic of my own ocean before all the birds would die and so that I could once again swim in the sea. I had polluted 80 per cent of birds with the unnamed flows of my thoughts. Birds had received on average 31 plastic parts inside of them. Naturalness was therefore mixed with the unnatural. All the beautiful and good things had become frightening.

Salt water, sun and waves scattered plastic into nanoparticles, impossible for the eye to see. These nanoparticles penetrated into fishes, between the copuscles and tissues, causing inflammation.

This was the beginning of the cancer mechanism that had destroyed my ability to love and be loved.

Could I still get back this island of mine? Maybe I could create a hammock out of all that waste and it could bear me and waste could be in use after all. The hammock would come to the island with me and I could see how the dew of heavens would collect on its surface and lick all the salt away from its surface. But first I should catch those pieces of plastics. Life was still totally identified in me. I could do this. Surely I could not get all the plastic waste of the ocean, but certainly I would be alerted to collect them as they came ashore. In doing so I would save the chance to be me. I would save the chance to be us.

> The colors fades from path of the traveller,
> tears will finally be broken.
> You will not attempt to hold on anymore,
> but you will open up your heart:
> it can now blow through the nets of the summer.
>
> You are not old yet, even if you feel so.
> There are many crosses to carry,
> even if the graveyard is quiet.
> The dust turns into a diamond,
> the memory of man.
>
> And the rays of the sun cry out,
> they shine on your eyes both silent and loud.
> You will not notice it,
> how fades
> the colors from the path of the traveller.
>
> You drank your libation secretly,
> You stepped it deep into the field.
> You dove through the dark,
> echo replied, replied only:
> there are just questions, too many.
>
> It does not matter what you have,
> not even what you once had.
> What is in me, that is real:
> Open your heart.
>
> Let the clean water flow through it!

Lapland

The moon fell into its thoughts and sprinkled them along the shore of heaven for the sun to take it all behind the mountains in Lapland. The mountain stood in place as you were watching, but as you turned your back it always moved its peak further away. The mysterious soul under the blanket of snow, in blind spot of untravelled paths.

Three reindeer dug under the snow, looking for something to eat in the yard of a residential house. Those animals of the forest were at home, and that´s where they really were. The man had built his house for their land. The builder of the house thought that he owned the reindeer too. I guess it was some kind of solace for this poor soul of the human being.

Bright pink and purple danced in the sky above it all. The dance of the colours invited one to rest and watch silently, how the snow and the water, side by side, guided the river to flow at the feet of the Laplandic mountain. You could never know beforehand when the trusted road would be closed with the reindeer fence. Closed by someone else.

I turned back. I sought the north with my eyes, turned my head toward the east, south and west. I did it for so long that I finally understood how to listen to all the reflections on the fragmented paths of the moon and on the roads of the sun.

Pakasaivo

I looked at the steep slope which protected the lake from the flows of the rivers. Only a small rivulet trickled to the lake but other than that groundwater fountains sang the water for the lake. Today was calm and full of silence.

It looked like an ordinary lake, but I knew it was very different. At a depth of twelve and a half meters the composition of the water was full of hydrogen suphide, anoxic. That deeper water kept everything within it, all the forms of origin.
On the bottom of the lake were all the sunken boats with the oars. There were all the logs, on which I had been playing. It had been so easy to stand on them and to roll them around on the surface of the water as I had when I'd been young. The lake was 50 meters above the surface of the deeper water. And I knew that I should honor the lake rather than fear it.

There was no seasonal turnover between the surface water and groundwater within a year. The proper term for a lake such as this was a meromictic lake. The clear water stayed clear on the top of the lake and hydrogen sulphide-containing water stayed in the depths as it was. The water of the lake did not confuse things indiscriminately, and it did not create unimaginable reactions for things that happened.

In a human being something like this would never be possible. Some of the Lapps believed that they could live inside the clear water if they would live the sinless life, while others believed that the devil itself lived on this lake. Pakasaivo reminded me strongly that the same feeling could be both right and wrong, depending on the target of the feeling, the situation and the way of bringing it up. The feeling was by no means always right, even though so many people claimed it to be so. Not even then, although the feeling itself feels real, true, and justified.

Some believes that this magical lake is 60 meters deep, while others believe that it has only intermediate bottom. No hard bottom could be found, the bottom gives in. It is as the human skin, which feels the way of the touch and transmits a signal of it to the whole being.

My grandmother believed that Saivo people lived in Pakasaivo. According to her, Saivo people lived happily upside down on the other side of the lake. And after all, even I carried my grandmother within my own being, even though I did not think about it or remember it all the time.

People of Lapland had sacrificed reindeer for the lake, had worshipped it. But I knew that I wanted more than today or tomorrow; I wanted more life than death and the past.

I walked on the south side of the beach. Mansonite rock of the north rose up to 40 meters abruptly, then continued its dive under the surface of the water. The wall of the rock reflected its shadows and faces on the surface of the lake. I sat down thoughtfully on the stone of the southern shore and sagged my feet in the water.

Preacher

Time passed. I wandered in the wilderness of Lapland until I was exhausted. It seemed to me that I would never get out of this wilderness. My skin was salty for several days and my throat was too rough to form words. One day a man walked towards me, he was dressed in a worn, tattered robe. *"Banish sorrow from your heart and to fight the suffering of flesh; for youth and the dawn of life are vanity."* The man was a preacher. I wondered how I could banish grief and injustice from my thoughts. How could I live without yearning for the past and without waiting and fearing the future?

However, the preacher knew my thoughts, for he was a wise man. He offered me water. As I drank from the preacher´s wineskin, he said to me: *"Sow your seed in the morning, and do not rest your hand until evening; because you do not know what will prosper, whether this or that, or whether both will be equally good."* This is how it was, I had to drink, and to sow the true way of thinking and action, which would lead to concrete good. I had been selfish, the salt on my skin knew it very well. Selfishness had led me to do wrong, therefore, my ears echoed curses and accusations. Proper and true water could give me ability to form words again and pure water would eliminate the salt from my skin so it could heal.

I could not change the choices I had made. So I knelt down in front of the preacher and tears fell down from my eyes. The preacher knew I was saying how sorry I am. The preacher touched my chin and lifted my head to the sky. I felt and knew that I was forgiven. For the first time in years, I knew for sure that I was free and I would be also be free to choose the right thing in different situations.

As I would base my choices on unselfish love and justice and would do everything with respect and humbly, the choice could not be that bad.

I closed my eyes and I felt how the wilderness disappeared around me and how it rained on my skin. In my soul I saw how green seedlings grew through my skin and a dove flew towards the sky out of my mouth. I opened my eyes to see this reality and for this moment I was finally able to say, "Thank you."

He creates everything to be new

Meeting with preacher was a strong and deep experience. It gave me strength for a long time. In spite of the forgiveness something in me was still hidden, down in the deepest gorges.

After the summer, autumn arrived in all its blaze of color. But eventually all the colors faded and dropped to the earth. There were leaves on the ground. Brown leaves. Darkened ugly leaves. I escaped to meet the autumn, and I trampled the leaves on the path as I walked. The sky was still unfrozen and it dropped its rays and drops on my face.

Time passed. I had not payed any attention to leaves for a while. Naturally the spring opened my eyes for a moment to see the new buds on bare branches. But after that I had not paid them much attention. Sometimes during the sunny days I noticed how the sun played on the green hair of the trees, but otherwise leaves had been dancing with the currents of the air without me noticing it. So often I drew my gaze only on the ground. Exactly what I was doing now.

Autumn had arrived, and gnawed at my mind. All the beauty and sexuality, which was created in me, was now beneath my the feet. The path was covered with dead leaves. I had lost the gift created in me. Part of it had been tried to be taken away, but in the end I had actually given it over to be forgotten.

I looked at the golden necklace I found in the forest, as it rested on the top of a fallen tree. It was forgotten there. It glinted beautifully on top of the soil. The same roots that had pulled the soil from undeground.

I woke up in silence and watched, no one would see. In my mind I stepped next to the roots. I sat down and I felt as I would be a fairy of the forest. I whispered into my hands: "You are worthy," and I stroked my wet and matted hair with my hand. Megalith loosened itself from the rock, and plumped down for the embrace of the moss. Black ravens flew over behind the meglith, they flew over the trees, out of my forest. I laid my fingers down on top of the golden necklace, feeling its pulsation in my soul.

Everything I saw disappeared from my eyes, but the birds were singing inside of me. He created everything again, to be new.

Under the snow

The winter period had arrived once again to Lapland. Slender and thin sheets of birch bark curled into a roll and were given direction by the wind to roll around and around, over the landscape of thousands of glittering snow diamonds.

I felt an invisible presence on my shoulder: "Child, here is a grain of happiness, just right here." I stopped to see the trees and top of the trees more clearly. I wanted to see the roots beneath the ground, so I had to close my eyes. Right here is a grain of happiness.

Some trees can be planted, while others can be grown only from seed. So if you want the tree get the proper roots; as tree species roots with a strong main root should not break. Perhaps in me, during my life has been a bit of both kinds of trees, but in this moment it did not matter, because the wind could carry, wherever it wanted and I was able hear now what it whispered.

I looked under the snow and below the bent trees. I looked at the trees that had fallen and at the wind-torn branches. There were so many memories on my skin. And yet right here, is a grain of happiness. I get to walk on my path from early morning till the evening, and that, is good.

Where would the journey lead me before the final goal, I could not know. I could not honestly say that I fully understood and knew even my own steps taken on this path. But just right here and right now – that was enough. I had escaped, and found my hiding place.

At the fountain

Water over the path

The well-known path was filled with water. Roots of the trees wanted to wash themselves and take messages forward. The path was no longer just a path which is passing in one direction but now it allowed the water to flow over.

It was like the subconscious would have found its way into the feelings, creating its own marks for the complex system of thoughts, giving meaning to things. This well-known path had to open up to pass through this day, into the future.

Ice started to melt, water flowed. Small grains of sand settled in new positions. It was like a postural treatment, which takes nausea away. The granules just had to get resettled after their precipitation. Then freedom flowed over my being, covered me with opportunities.

How much had my subconscious been influenced from my own roots, how much had I inherited the same emotional landscapes that had been handed down from generation to generation? How much I could explore and discover new things about myself? How well, now, could I draw a map of myself? How well could I get to know myself by understanding my loved ones in past generations?

But water already flowed over the path, and I ran happily through the flowing water. It was time to get my toes wet!

Water of the fountain

The water rose up to the surface under the sand. It rose up bright and fresh, clean enough to drink. This water did not let the ice and snow to cover itself because it was actually a life-giving force. It was a soul in me, who would live as long as I would live.

It was called Runeberg´s source, not without reason. You can find your way there through art and poetry. It can not be fully explained, and never fully understood. But it can be identified completely, and felt within emotions. So much truer than true, than the steps taken before it.

The edges of the trees reflected from the surface of the source. Branches cast dark shadows on the water's surface, never being able to physically touch the surface of it or the depths of underground. The waters' surface revealed everything both above and below. Green plants showed up to the surface, as you just stopped at the scene to view it. A passerby would able to see it as clearly as he was able to see the shadows of the trees. Roots of the plants with different colours created ripples on bottom of the fountain, as if it were a multifaceted brain, that man could hardly know. However, all of it was laid bare, visible for him to whom it was shown.

I whispered my fragile, hope-filled prayer:

"I will reveal everything for you now. You'll be close to the landscape of my soul for as long as you want, because you are also sharing yours. Trees were swaying from side to side and wind brought rippling to the surface of the fountain. However, the soul is always present with a new, fresh water. Holy God has created this in me and you. He has allowed me and you to to meet up on this bridge and by this fountain by his mercy. This is something from Himself, something within me and you. Uspeakably beautiful and refreshing. So full of life.

I see your smile, I see your cries, I see your fear. I share it all, even though it all can not be touched. I can not take it to be mine and I can not give it to be yours. But as the surface of water is part of the fountain and surface of the water lies beside the air.

And as the shadows of the trees are stuck to the surface of the fountain: the same way I am within us now. We do not have to be afraid of this; this is how it should be. We see ourselves and we see each other. The passage on the path with all the turns, events and waitings have worth it all, so I could get to the fountain and finally to be ready to build this bridge."

The fountain bubbled its water. I watched how the leaves waved silently with the movements of the water on the bottom of the fountain. Grains of sand leaped and competed with each other and my mind wandered along the surface of the water. I admired the shadows of the trees and smile of the clouds floating in the other reality which was reflected on the surface. How beautiful is the fresh bubbling water which comes through the sand!

In my mind you touched my hand and kissed me softly on my shoulder. I bent my back and my hair tickled the surface of the water and you held my hands. You held me firmly and securely. The landscape looked so different in this view.

I got up and kissed you. Water dropped from my hair to your shirt and I dove to rejoice with your soul through your eyes. I stroked your thoughts and your skin; paradise opened itself for us. Within this loving, open, and sensitive atmosphere, we were truly in presence. The flowers opened up petals widely around the fountain and fairies rose to from the bottom of the fountain to dance through our bodies.

I experienced how the water filled the grooves on my face and the sand filled calluses on my feet. "Honest and bare, respect who you really are," you whispered in my ear. My life and your life twisted and mixed with the histories of our families and with all the dreams of this moment. We did know it all, yet perhaps we will never understand it all. We could never achieve all we want and there would be parts of things we would come to understand to not be worth trying to reach. But right now, together, we dove for this rejuvenating and free joy.

I cried to see my courage; to dream of such a bare love. I did not want to ever let go of this dream.

In the meddle of the dark

I immersed myself in the bubbling of the fountain and I let my mind release from everything else. Darkness outside drove off the last glows of the day. There was an increasingly darkening blue area with a few pale flame in the middle of the blackness. Water whispered in my ear in a language that I could not explain.

I could feel now how my back began to grow wings. They penetrated up under my shoulder blades, then grew to their full potential: light, fluffy, and beautiful.
My toes also got to experience something completely new as the small bones and joints were filled with glowing fire, which illuminated my way. I rose up in the air from the fountain and flew on the edges on a black sky. I did not look down at the land with its busy people, I was floating forward face up and eyes closed. My toes directed my way, my hair grabbing the gold particles as I went.

I spread my hair wide open with my fingers. The northern lights glided the sky in different colors, purely for the joy of those who dare to see the wonderful colours of timeless dreams, even in the midst of all the darkness.

Distant echoes were heard behind the ports of sleep.
Meadows filled with flowers, willed up with pure white snow
and with blood that makes you live:
I saw something secret, something Holy.
Although I knew very well that all of this
is only a small reflection of the greater.

I pressed my lips against each other,
to feel even better how small I am.
Shattering power went through me
and my skin was flowing with colors to my fingertips
by creating my dreams to be images and a set of songs.
I knew I was here and now,
also my dream would be here and now.

I raised my head, with all that was in it, and raised my hands:
I do not have any more than this,
but so much is what there is.
And I knew at that moment,
that the Creator knew everything.
And I knew at that moment,
that the Creator could be everything.

I was so completely seen
and my desires were so perfectly consulted:
I felt dizzy of His infinite love
and His infinite power to create anew
and to create beauty.
And my eyes were able to hear the echoes,
when I truly believed, knowing the truth,
even if it seems to be impossible.

AT THE BRIDGE

The carrier of fire

Fire and water were next to the other.

We watched the fire fighters and bubbling of the water. We heard how the fire consumed the wood, smelled the smoke, and we felt the heat on our skin. We heard the gurgle of the water.

Fire and water, seen as the fundamental characteristic of essence. Can even supercritical water ingite a fire, let alone acquire fire by itself? But the souls of the dead water bears. We lay down our loved ones with lilies to continue their journey to where we cannot go. I, myself, am however the stream, the conduit, where the memories of loved ones continues their path, until I will get to see for myself what there is, after my own life down here.

I hold your hand and observe how the furrows of our hands attach us to each other. You are the power of my initiative, the force that creates the will to be present in this life, as long as it is bestowed to us.

Eyelids

You stroked my eyelids timidly and quietly. I whispered thousands of trees songs in your ear. The field of thistles was silent. You heard me.

The grass of the lawn bowed, bowed to the flowers, to the starry sky and studied its own roots. I remembered the phrase I had learnt a long ago: "Osmosis is the diffusion of the water through the semi-permeable membrane".

That's what this really was, to see from many perspectives, the shared scenery of souls. I fell into a refreshing sleep. I would be valuable for me, as I am. Just as I am.

Both he and she realized that they had created new vivid colors within their blanket. A sleep invited them to swing between different realities. A swing was rocking by the climbing plants. Through fluttering moths they learnt new things and new languages.

The frozen roses of the garden were beautiful. Floating fishes rested, in peace. Still, it was spring, and the living diamonds sparkled with laughter around and bent themselves into absurd positions. These were the diamonds of my rooms - I smiled proudly.

Turquoise ships arrived in the port. I arrived home from the sea. I had seen and experienced a lot. I knew very well that the sea can not anchor a ship permanently – the sea was never meany to do so. I was aware that it was necessary to travel timelessly. Moving yet being still as you travelled down the paths of water, the blind spots of the forest and within the dances of the airflows. At last I had found my joy of the harvest!

Internal resonance

My shoulders had carried so many worries and troubles. Some had been sadness without mourning. Some of it had adhered fast along the journey. But you were willing to touch me again. You were ready to touch me this way, as if for the first time. The way it used to be, you had massaged me with a mechanical touch, as you were deep in your thoughts. But now you felt the tension of my muscles, you felt the location of my bones and felt the touch of your own palm on my skin. You did not cause bruises by poking or scratching or stretching my skin. You were fully in the presence of the moment. You resounded me for the first time.

Your respecting, encouraging words enhanced within me the person I had been created to be. The air flowed freely inside me and the sound was amplified through my bones. I am made from your rib, I knew it now very well.

We are no longer just each other's echo, who repeat it all senselessly from outside without hearing and feeling the true vibration. We are part of the same chords of the melody, we can be sung both in harmony together and separately.

You look at me with your fingertips,
you touch the inner me with the listening of your ear.
We will carry on within this warmth,
as the external world gives birth to iceflakes.

Here and now, faces
the lifetime paths of two human beings,
the soul dressing scars can be made beautiful.
Here and now we cross our hands.
Now it is time to be us.

My lips feels your thoughts.
I smell deep feelings from your skin.
We float in the sky, swamp as a cover beneath us.
Soft scent of the cranberries as a memory,
when we are apart from the duties.
to experience what it is now to be us.

Arched bridge

We had traveled our journeys. We had gone through our own internal deserts and seas. We had faced the animals of the forests and the mossy paths. We had swam in the river and walked along its banks. Now it was time to stop. Now we were able to see on the side of the river that was between.

Now it was time to build a new bridge. The old suspension bridge was hopelessly collapsed over the time by the raging wind. No one could save himself doing anything else than grabing its rails – we had not known it then. In a moment, years ago, it had collapsed under us and drifted away from us for the river to carry on.

However, now we were right here. Older than ever before. We were more sure than ever before. Still, we were naked as newborn babies. We were ready to build a strong bridge. We knew how the water would rise higher and higher from time to time. We knew now how the water flows under the bridge – it would not be needed otherwise. We would not cross the bridge just to pass each other, knew now how to marvel at the passage of the water and avoid drowning in it anymore.

We carefully chose the stones that we needed. Durable stones, because we were not going to build a decorative arch, but an ordinary bridge, which would support us from day to day. We would build an arched bridge where the highest stone unites the two sides with perfect symmetry. After all, the highest stone is the main stone in whole bridge. *It is the perfect love that casts out fear.* That is what is needed when day turns to blackness around us, the wind blows its cry from the depths of the sea, and the animals of the forest gather to drink on the riverside invisible but sensed.

We held each other's hands and looked at the sky, bowed our heads towards the river. We turned ourselves towards each other and until we saw our souls. We sensed unity as we kissed, on top of the highest stone of our bridge.

Under the skin

When you lift the veil from your face,
you feel how the amount of water increases under my skin,
how the amount of water to rises under our feet.

You see clearly once again,
like a child sees clearly.
Feel free to hold my hand.

When tragedy evaporates from your eyes,
you feel, how the amount of water increases under your skin,
how the amount of water rises under our feet.

I will go with you,
through all the mire.
You hold on to life.

When I take the answers from my lips,
I know how much the water increases under your skin,
how much it rises under our feet.

I see or I do not see,
but I hear more clearly, your emotions,
I share your genuine thoughts.

When our faces reflect the experiences.
When we walk our bare course.
When love grows in freedom:
Man encountered in being,
vulnerability respected
under our skin.

Becoming united forest

Just as before, the same two forests grew next to each other: pine and birch. As the sun was shining, the birch forest shone in its whiteness, with only the black shadows between the trees and black stripes of the birch bark. Likewise, the pine forest underlined the brown structure and firm structure of trunks in the sunlight.

During an overcast day, the pine forest seemed ordinary, even slightly depressing. The birch Forest mixed the white and black to be gray, as there would be nothing to say.

Years went by, and the trees of the forest strengthened. Greenish moss grew on the pine trees, up from the soil to be part of the darkening bottom of their trunks. Birch Trees spread their curved branches high above. The branches were like wrinkles of the aged, the enmeshment of thoughts.

These two forests next to each other blended their trees. Birches settled in front of the pine forest next to the road and pine trees protected those young trees with their strong and firm trunks. The color spectrum of the sun's rays played on the tops of the trees but an observer could only guess at the trails of the roots deep in the soil. It was our home-forest. We knew that within this forest we would receive have all that we needed: plenty of oxygen, water and food.

Disappearing echoes of the dreams of yesterdays,
sand paper is smooth at last.
I bend my toes in the water
and yawn listlessly.
I listen to whispers of secrets
and blow soap bubbles,
fill up my backyard.

There is no hurry anymore,
because summer has arrived
and the wells are filled with water.
What is a human being to be,
loved as they are.

Birch branches like pinwheels
can be fit to the vase,
and I can border with moss
the edges of the beds.
Watch it all in your eyes,
and feel the dreams of your skin.

The smell of the salt on fingertips
creates a taste of life.
We laugh at each other's smiles
with our look.

Afterword

Towards me the map was drawn even stronger, the same I had been exploring at the beginning of my journey.

This map, whose existence I remembered as I briefly paused behind a Venetian blind, watching the childrens' play.

>When the mind´s arcs
>are running out tears
>at the gates of the soul,
>angels are waiting.
>With open arms they welcome
>the seekers of motherland
>who are lost in tic-tac belled forest
>where stoned metal pieces
>have forgotten to be treasures of traveller.
>
>Water rises up from the flow
>to praise the heavens
>and to admire clouds
>whom are reaching to offer food for hungry
>from the banquet table of the air flow
>with new containers.
>
>No one wants to be away
>from that moment.
>
>No one whom have dared to swallow the chip
>of the mirrors reflection.
>or whom have drunk own outlines from the water level.
>´Cause the whole of oneself
>is the biggest evidence of human being.
>
>That is when all the wounds
>are revealed to identify
>and all the odysseys will get their names
>at the chain of the memories.
>Every meaningful meeting and abandonment
>will rest in peace at the furrows of the hands.

That is time when hair
can flutter in the air
and it will bring dew drops for the skin.
Is it only this life
between birth and death?
Or did there appear a living plant after all?

Yes,
the wind brought a seed for the cold water.
Dew gave a birth for it
and the heat fostered it for ownership.
To be in everyone´s lips as meeting.
To be a guide for travellers of midnight.
To encourage those who are hiding in darkness.
To be a composer for those who have forgotten
the songs of their names.

All of this is one of the victories of brightness:
the celebration of the starry sky and our solar system.

www.ingramcontent.com/pod-product-compliance
Lightning Source LLC
Chambersburg PA
CBHW042309150426
43198CB00001B/12